Chasing God and the Kids Too

Balancing a Mom's Most Important Pursuits

Cheryl R. Carter

Revell
Grand Rapids, Michigan

© 2006 by Cheryl R. Carter

Published by Fleming H. Revell
a division of Baker Publishing Group
P.O. Box 6287, Grand Rapids, MI 49516-6287

Printed in the United States of America

Library of Congress Cataloging-in-Publication Data
Carter, Cheryl R.
  Chasing God and the kids too : balancing a mom's most important
pursuits / Cheryl R. Carter.
      p.   cm.
  Includes bibliographical references.
  ISBN 10: 0-8007-3110-7 (pbk.)
  ISBN 978-0-8007-3110-6 (pbk.)
    1. Mothers—Religious life. 2. Motherhood—Religious
aspects—Christianity. I. Title.
  BV4529.18.C38 2006
  248.8′431—dc22   2005025106

To my Lord and Savior, Jesus Christ,
who never runs away from me
but has always passionately pursued me
every day of my life!

Contents

Foreword by Derek G. Carter   9
Introduction: Why God Created Mothers   11
So Why Am I Here?

1. Playing Catch Me If You Can   15
   Pursuing God, but Is He Really Running Away?
2. The Most Unlikely Place to Start   20
   Organizing Your Home
3. Maintaining Your Momentum   44
   Implementing a Realistic Schedule
4. As a Mother Thinketh, So Is She   66
   Having Peaceful, Practical, and Productive Thoughts
5. Is It Really Possible?   89
   How to Really Have a Consistent Quiet Time
6. Catching Up with God   110
   In His Presence, the Exhilaration of the Chase
7. Follow the Leader   127
   Playing "Mommy Says" on the Mountain
8. Passing the Baton   149
   Let the Children Come—Allowing the Kids to Join in the Chase

Contents

9. The Right Attitude 170
   Living in the Joy and Grace of the Moment
10. Do You Hear Him? 190
    Hearing God in Our Hearts and in Our Homes
11. The Finish Line 208
    Standing Strong Spirit, Soul, and Body
12. I Really Want to Know! 221
    Questions We All Ask

Resources 235

Foreword

"Hey, Mom, did you wash my sweat suit?"
"Mom, where are my ballet shoes?"
"Hon, have you seen my blue tie?"
"Mom, I'm hungry; when will dinner be ready?"
These are the cries heard in many households all the time. Mothers answer them every day. However, there is a cry that is not as loud as these, yet it occurs in every Christian home. This is a greater cry that mothers are often unable to answer.
"Come, let's talk."
"Come sit with me for a little while."
"Come and I will tell you some secrets."
These are the cries of our Father that mothers hear and desire to answer but aren't always able to respond to immediately. Imagine the frustration of hearing the cry of the Creator and not being able to answer. I do not mean to suggest that mothers don't spend any time in meaningful fellowship with the Lord. They do, but often the stress and time-consuming tasks of managing a home and everything else crowd out quality time with the Lord.

9

Often, in exasperation, mothers accept lost time with the Lord as the norm rather than the exception. But when you think about it, hearing from God is of paramount importance, especially when you're called to the awesome responsibility of managing and also nurturing a family. This responsibility requires a consistent and intimate relationship with the Lord.

I believe Cheryl to be the ideal mother to address this issue. Since the birth of our first child, I have seen Cheryl identify this issue and deal with it head-on. Utilizing practical ideas and personal self-determination, Cheryl has successfully nurtured a consistent and deeply committed personal relationship with the Lord. At the same time, she has poured herself into our children, nurturing them spiritually, mentally, emotionally, and physically, while also holding our marriage to a high standard. In essence, Cheryl has chased after God and the kids too and has caught up, and she is now running alongside of both!

Derek G. Carter

Introduction

Why God Created Mothers

So Why Am I Here?

Mothering is a funny term. It's a noun made into a verb, therein defining itself. It is all rather strange when you think about it. Am I endowed with some superior power just because I gave birth? I have often wondered about motherhood, so when my daughter wrote this poem, it provoked further thought for me.

The Reason God Created Mothers

God created mothers because he knew:

Only a mom could tell a monster to get out of your closet
and he leaves even though you know he's not really
there.

Only a mom could tell you a bleeding knee is going to be all right and you believe her even though you still see the blood oozing out.

Only a mom could crawl around the house with you on Sunday morning and help you find your church shoes even though you're positive you left them in your room under the bed.

Only a mom could talk to you when you're upset and tell you everything is going to be all right and you believe her even though you think it cannot ever be all right.

Only a mom would let you slip into bed with her and your dad after you had a bad dream and let you sleep there the whole night even though your little sister is there too.

Only a mom can make you put on a sweater because she's cold even though you're not cold and later you are glad you put it on.

Only a mom can tell you it's okay after you broke a crystal candy dish and you feel bad but she smiles as she sweeps up the pieces and asks if you want some candy.

But mainly I think God created mothers because he knew he was going to send his Son Jesus to earth and he knew a mother would know just what to do. . . . He also created mothers because he knew I needed one.

Janae J. Carter, age 9

As I read Janae's poem, I thought about all the times when I did not know what to do as a mom. How did Mary know how to respond to Christ when he was a child? Surely his miraculous birth and discussions with the rabbis (Luke 2:46) indicated he was indeed a special child. How did Elizabeth, the mother of John the Baptist, know how to raise him such that as an adult he was able to be such a radical voice for change in his society? What did Timothy's mother and grandmother do that caused Paul to remark that the same faith he saw in Timothy he had initially seen in his mother, Eunice, and grandmother, Lois?

All of these mothers drew their strength from God. They learned at his feet what to do and how to raise their children. They maintained continual communion with their Creator. This is what all mothers need

Mary made a decision to sit at the Master's feet. She made a good decision. We can too.

to do. In fact, this is what all Christian mothers want to do. Yet it is hard for us; we are often distracted by dirty dishes, whining children, and our endless to-do lists.

We are at times overwhelmed with ministering to the needs of our family. But we can sit at the feet of Jesus. We can make the right choice. Martha was distracted, but Mary made a decision to sit at the Master's feet. She made a good decision. We can too. This decision is often predicated on our having our home in order, having the right attitude, and exercising spiritual discipline.

Join me as I chase after God, as I relentlessly pursue his presence and show you how you too can nurture your family and still spend quality time with God. Every good runner must be prepared for a race. Come. Put on your running shoes. Lace them up. Run in place as we thank God for meeting you in these pages. Ready. Set. Let's go!

Prayer

Lord, help me to see you!

1

Playing Catch Me If You Can

Pursuing God, but Is He Really Running Away?

I looked at my Day-Timer; I had missed morning devotions again! The house was a mess, and Jarrett's T-shirt was encrusted with bananas. Yet I was invited to a women's prayer meeting, and I was determined to go. I had rarely sat through an entire sermon since Jarrett's birth. So I chose to forget about the overflowing hamper, the mountain of dishes, and the adhesive kitchen floor. At that moment, more than anything else, I knew I needed to be at that prayer meeting. And I was on my way!

As I arrived, "This is the day that the Lord has made" echoed from the sanctuary. My heart leaped as I joined in the chorus. Joyfully humming along, I checked Jarrett into the nursery and secured paddle number seven. Then I slipped in the sanctuary, crossed over a few women, and sat on the second pew as the chorus refrained even louder. "I will rejoice and be glad in it." I closed my eyes and began to sing. Softly, solemnly, slowly, and ever so worshipfully and thankfully I sang, "Yes, I will rejoice and be glad in it."

A few choruses later, a tap on the shoulder interrupted my touch with eternity. The woman behind me pointed to the woman in the bright red dress frantically waving the number seven paddle. I made my way to the nursery to retrieve Jarrett, who seemed inconsolable. Concerned nursery workers flanked about him, looking frustrated. His face brightened as I reached out to him. As I flung him on my hip, the relieved elderly nursery staff grinned. "He just wanted his mommy." I put on my very best fake Christian smile for appearances, but actually I was downright angry.

I was angry with myself for being angry with Jarrett. I was angry with God for allowing my worship time to be interrupted. I was angry with my husband, Derek, because, well, he was the easiest one to be angry with—besides, I didn't feel guilty about being angry with him, at least not at that moment. My emotions were all topsy-turvy and very much conflicted.

Suffering through years of infertility, I had longed to be a mother. Now the very role I had pleaded with God to give me was separating me from him. Intellectually, I knew that rationalization was wrong, but at the moment it sure seemed right. The guilt was overwhelming; I felt bad that I resented Jarrett and at the same time was upset with myself for having inconsistent quiet or devotional time. So how could I expect God to help me? I reasoned.

All I wanted was God. I just wanted to know he was there. My heart longed to touch God, but it felt like he was running away: playing a game of "catch me if you can." Other moms had told me to just accept that I couldn't do the same spiritual gymnastics I had done before I was a mother. I had been known to get up earlier than God himself and pray down holy fire. Well, at least that's the way I remembered it. It was the overflow of my quiet time that had enabled me to teach, pray, and give an encouraging word when needed. I just could not accept that that aspect of my life was now long gone because I had embraced the call to motherhood.

> **"Come near to God and he will come near to you."**
> **James 4:8**

Being a mother was a calling, a divine calling. That was undeniable. I knew that. I also knew I needed God more than ever to help me walk out that calling. I had tried reading devotional books, revamping my schedule, getting up earlier, going to bed later, but nothing worked. The things I read were all so structured and written by such perfect Christians. They did not seem to address the emotional and time constraints of mothers with young children. Those resources offered little help.

Missing out on the women's prayer meeting magnified my frustrations with my spiritual growth. I came home, threw the diaper bag on the floor, and sat on it, consumed with pity and indignation. Still looking for a lifeline, I flipped through Derek's Bible, which was still right there on the floor where I had dropped it as I was rushing out to the meeting. I opened it up to James 4:8: "Come near to God and he will come near to you."

Inwardly, I felt like yelling, "God, I am trying to draw near to you, but you keep running away!" But I had what I would term enough religious restraint or just sheer fear not to say what I was really feeling. This was not necessarily a good thing. Ever so gently, the thought occurred to me that perhaps I needed to be real with God. I was a lousy mom, at best a mediocre Christian, a terrible homemaker, and a lackluster wife, I thought as I kicked the splattered Legos from under my foot. I waited for the fire of heaven to fall. Silence . . . well, except for the plinking of Jarrett throwing the Legos on the floor.

God did not accept the invitation to my pity party; instead, a thought faintly occurred to me. Perhaps I needed

> I had to be proactive and creative in my pursuit to know God better. I couldn't do things in the tradition-prescribed way.

to run after God. The thought resounded in my head. Right there I began to softly sing, "This is the day the Lord has made." I was a bit off-beat and off-key, but it didn't matter. It wasn't long before ever so gently I could sense God's presence. And guess what? It didn't seem like he was angry with me. In that little step of praising him, I had drawn close to him.

Well, I reasoned, if a little thing like singing his praises and being honest would draw me near, what other things could I do to draw me into God's presence? Who said I needed to sit at a table and read the Bible? I had received revelation while straddling a diaper bag on the floor among the crumbs and Legos. Instead of transposing my frustrations on God and others, I needed to develop a new mindset. I had to be proactive and creative in my pursuit to know God better.

I couldn't do things in the tradition-prescribed way. Books filled my shelves, but none of them understood my frustration of wanting to serve God fervently, yet being too pooped to do it in a structured or traditional way. But I knew God understood me. He would guide me in my spiritual growth while I addressed the challenges of motherhood.

I was determined to grow close to God and to be a better mom. Right there in my home, I could make changes that would help me get to know God better. I could chase God! This paradigm shift was freeing. The more I thought about it, the clearer it became. I could chase after God. I merely had to find creative ways to pursue him and at the same time gracefully grow in my calling as a mother.

This thought released me from all the guilt I had amassed from unread devotional books, Proverbs 31 sermons, unrealistic schedules, and yes, even the missed prayer meeting.

I could minister to my family and pursue God at the same time. Wow! One does not necessarily negate the other. I could do both. It was not an either-or deal. I could be a strong Christian, a loving wife, an effective homemaker, and a godly mother.

Chasing God is obviously a misnomer, because God never runs away from us.

God was not running away from me; he was simply stirring me to join in the chase. Chasing God is obviously a misnomer, because God never runs away from us. He is always in hot pursuit of us. I began to see him differently.

Do you see him? Catch that glimmer in his eye and the beckoning hand. He bids us to come near. Grab your running shoes. Lace them up. Tie them tight. Place your foot on the starting line. See him? Ready. Set. Let's go!

Prayer

Lord, grace me to run after you with fervor.

19

2

The Most Unlikely Place to Start

Organizing Your Home

Learning how to organize a home just doesn't seem like a logical place to begin the chase. It doesn't seem spiritual enough. After all, what's so spiritual about scrubbing crud out of a dirty toilet? Yet organizing your home is the best place to begin, because our homes must be in order before we can deal seriously with any spiritual discipline. Have you ever tried to pray seriously in a cluttered room or been distracted by the filth on the carpet as you worshipfully bowed during your quiet time? A clean and orderly home really is essential to spiritual growth.

You cannot get your inner life in order when your outer life is a mess. I've learned over the years that when it comes to mothers, there's one thing we need more than anything else, but few of us would admit it. We need to control our environment. Don't get me wrong; control is not an inherently bad thing, because mothers typically are controlled by so many other things—the dirty laundry, the meals, the late-night soccer games. They all scream out for our attention.

> **You cannot get your inner life in order when your outer life is a mess.**

Everything vies for our time and tries to control us. We instinctually feel the urge to take back the reins. Every mom knows what I'm talking about. We carry our children in us for forty weeks, and they spend the next six years learning to detach themselves. We nurse them day and night. They sit in our laps or cling to our hips while we're cooking dinner. Inquisitive preschoolers camp at the bathroom door until we come out. Even though the umbilical cord was cut at birth, our children spend six years getting used to the idea. I am not whining, just stating my case for why we crave control.

Actually, nearly everyone wants to control something. It is part of our fallen nature. But it isn't long after we bring that baby home from the hospital that we discover he or she controls us. And so the struggle begins. I make this point because over the years in my time-management and organizing workshops (relax, I'm not one of those neat freaks; I am a recovering "messie" myself, and I think I won't be completely cured until my last child goes off to college), I've found mothers need to get some control of their environment before they can seriously deal with inner issues of spiritual growth.

Be honest with me. Aren't there times when the dirty dishes keep you from sitting at the feet of Jesus? Or the furry orange-sized lint ball on the carpet distracts you even as you worshipfully bow your knee to give God glory? I know it does me! Denial gets us nowhere. We must deal with the problem. Some might say, why not go to Jesus first and ask him how to clean and organize our homes? It sounds so spiritual. But the truth is, for most of us, he has been speaking to us, and we just need to heed his words.

Your Home Should Serve You—You Should Not Serve It!

We think better and more clearly in a clean and orderly environment. I guess I should explain why I am dealing with the home. While you can be anywhere and grow spiritually, it is primarily the home where moms spend the most time. Right? Therefore, it seems rather logical to begin here.

Gifted, organized women should still stick around to hear what I have to say about organization, because often I see two kinds of Christian moms. The first spends all her time keeping the home immaculate. You could eat off the kitchen floor—not that you would ever want to, but she takes great pride in the cleanliness of her home. This mom finds her identity in a house to be admired by others. Her perfectionist tendencies also keep her away from things of eternal value.

God does value a mom who diligently serves her family out of love and appreciates a home that reflects that, but I am talking about cleaning to such excess that the relationships with children and husband are marginalized. If the lines in your carpet are perpendicular to one another and your children's clothing is marked by the days of the week, then I'm talking to you. These moms need to be encouraged that God loves them no matter what they do, because frequently they are caught in the performance mode.

The other Christian mom I have observed is the go-with-the-flow type. She cannot find a pencil to take down a telephone number, so she uses her toddler's crayons. Of course, the toddler has scribbled on the wall and everything else with mom's missing pen. The dirty dishes and piled-up laundry don't seem to bother these ladies—well, actually they do, but somewhere along the way discouragement set in, and these moms just gave up on ever having an orderly home. They need lots of encouragement—and pens—to know things can change. They may feel buried

22

and burdened by their responsibilities and need someone to come along and give them help and hope.

Balance is the key. In both of the above cases, the moms serve their home. Both spend inordinate time keeping or attempting to keep the house neat. Neither the messy mom nor the orderly mom feels the freedom to leave the house alone and move on to higher pursuits. One is trapped by her perfectionism, and the other is overwhelmed by her disorganization. It's a shame both end up serving their homes when their homes should serve them. As long as they persist in those modes, they'll never be able to sit at the feet of Jesus unfettered by it all.

Now I know what you're thinking: it's the old Martha and Mary syndrome again. Remember, Mary sat at the feet of Jesus while Martha busied herself with household tasks. We sing songs like, "Don't be a Martha, so busy, busy all the time." I think Martha gets a bad rap. Let me explain. I understand Martha. If Jesus were coming to my house, you better believe I'd be running around getting everything prepared and in order. Wouldn't you? Martha was not a person driven by works; she just made a wrong choice.

Martha had experience sitting at Jesus's feet. Look at the Scripture closely. Luke 10:39 reads, "Mary . . . also sat at Jesus' feet" (KJV)—implying it was a regular practice for Martha to sit at Jesus's feet. According to Luke 10:40, she was merely distracted. Martha was loved by Jesus (John 11:5). Martha ran to Jesus when he entered Bethany after Lazarus had died and demonstrated her faith and knowledge of the Word by stating she knew Jesus could raise Lazarus from the dead. She was anything but a flaky Christian. She knew the Word.

Many of us have wrong perceptions of Martha. The truth is, all of us have been like Martha—distracted by our homes. Martha was a godly woman who had experienced sitting at Jesus's feet. She merely made a bad decision, distracted by everything that had to be done in the house. We too make bad decisions. Only God makes all the right decisions all the time. He is order because he authored order.

When God created the heavens and earth, he set everything in order. That order dictated the purpose for creation. In other words, the fish is made to conform perfectly to the water. The blue jay glides through the sky, while the peacock, though a bird, takes pride in strutting his stuff. Every creation has a purpose, and design validates that purpose. Even Adam and Eve were anatomically different due to the different assignments God had called each to do. This same biblical principle can be applied to our homes.

Purpose Always Precedes Order

Each room in our home has a purpose, and when that purpose is violated, disorder occurs. For instance, I always get a chuckle in my organizing workshops when I say a dining room table is not a desk. But you and I know that if papers and mail are tossed haphazardly on it, it becomes a desk—rather, it becomes a mess. Anytime purpose is violated, disorder occurs.

I usually encourage workshop participants to fill out a chart (see the end of the chapter) in which they list every room and space (including the foyer) in their home and specify the purpose for the room. Purpose is important because our homes need to be purposeful if they are to remain in order. After you have written down the purpose in column one, then identify the activities that occur in that room. If too many different activities occur in a room, it's a candidate for disorder. Locate where activities constantly reoccur. For example, if family members are reading in six different rooms in the house, you might want to limit the reading to just two rooms, accommodating the reading

Household Tips

- Take all your family board games out of their boxes and put them in a large box or storage bin. Lay the boards flat in the box. Place each game's pieces in a plastic storage bag. No more lost pieces. This also keeps dangerous small pieces away from younger siblings.
- Schedule days when the whole family can clean the house. The work will go by faster with many hands. It's also an excellent opportunity for the older siblings to teach their younger siblings chores.
- Open your mail near a wastebasket. Discard junk mail immediately. Reduce junk mail by writing to Mail Preference Service, Direct Marketing Association, P.O. Box 643, Carmel, NY 10512.

space with appropriate shelving and lighting. This will reduce the disorder caused by books scattered all over the home.

Some moms have told me the concept of purpose is too deep for their already cluttered minds and they find it easier to first list the activities that occur in the room. After they have identified the activities, they're better able to determine the purpose of the room. Either way you choose, the chart is a helpful tool to restrict activities so they only occur in specified places.

Filling out the chart for your whole house may take awhile, especially if you have multiple activities going on in various rooms. It's worth the time investment. Even my orderly friends like this sheet because it cuts down on their cleaning by limiting the different activities in each room. Most mothers like the concept of purpose.

Purpose is unique to each family. For instance, in my kitchen we have a rather large wipe board, and I used to have a place for the kids' toys because the purpose of my kitchen was to encourage me to cook meals. Cooking is not high on my list of favorite things to do. By having a wipe board in the kitchen, I could teach and cook at the same time. Or if the kids needed my assistance with a school question—and I always welcomed them into the kitchen—they could easily write the question on the board, especially if my hands were enmeshed in spaghetti sauce. I've found it is easier to get spaghetti sauce off a wipe board than off a school paper. The toys were there, likewise, so they would come in the kitchen and play while I was cooking.

I have spoken to a lot of moms who prefer cooking time to be their personal time. Naturally, the purpose of their kitchen would be different than my purpose. Get it? It's a very individual thing.

This simple exercise takes time, but once you have the concept down, you can easily adapt it even as your family changes. For instance, the purpose of my kitchen will change when my children pass their preteen years. Your purpose will change too as your family grows.

Involve your family in the process as you bring order to each room. Poll your kids. Ask them what they think the purpose of various rooms might be, then use their responses to help you focus on the purpose of each room. After you have determined the purpose of each room, you may then begin organizing the room. You will have to de-clutter first. You do this by going around the room clockwise with three bags labeled "Give Away," "Throw Away," and "Put Away." Be ruthless when throwing things away.

After you have de-cluttered, circle the room clockwise, organizing everything in sight. Put things away. Take note of what organizing items you need to make or purchase. Finally, circle the room clockwise a third time to clean it.

I can't get into all the facets of organizing, but this should provide a catalyst for you. Consider organizing your home a sacrament to your family. Serving our families is a service to God. While many of us know that, this realization is hard to grasp as we scrape burnt cheese off the smoking toaster or scrub the counter after our eight-year-old tried to make grilled peanut butter and turkey sandwiches. It's a matter of attitude. We must serve our families not out of drudgery but with godly resolve that we are fulfilling a higher purpose than just getting peanut butter oil off Formica.

Keeping the Family Moving Along

So let's, for the sake of argument, say your home is in order. By that I mean you can see the floor and a visitor has a reasonable path to each room without something falling on his or her head. No guilt, please. At times when I am consumed by projects, my house has looked like a condemned used-clothing store; but because I had systems in place, I would stop and address the problem as soon as the deadline blew over. That said, what every mom needs is a system to serve her household, and it is no less spiritual than spending time in prayer.

As I have struggled to maintain a household, I have discovered that managing a household involves an understanding of two key elements: inventory and maintenance. Everything we do falls into one of these categories. Inventory items keep the family moving and spontaneous. These items are their needs. They include food, clean clothes, electricity, and so on. I have to feed my children. They need to wear clean clothes. I have to pay the electricity bill, because I need lights. Most times these things cannot be delayed.

Maintenance items can be delayed. The kitchen floor may be sticky, but the family will still function. Your windows may be full of grime, but you can still see out of them. I don't advocate sticky floors or grimy windows, but I hope you get my point.

Inventory items should be taken care of first in your home. This will free you to address maintenance issues.

Clean Underwear and Socks Too!

One important inventory item is the laundry. This is a job with various steps. Often we neglect to think through the whole process; therefore, we do not complete the laundry in a one-time segment. Reduce the steps you take when doing laundry, and you'll see what I mean.

I hate doing laundry; therefore, I do it every day. No, it's not some redemptive, character-building, spiritual exercise. I simply hate dealing with the volume of laundry, so I try to do it every day so it doesn't pile up. With a husband who goes to the gym daily and active kids, this is actually quite easy for me.

Get help from others. Train little ones to sort the laundry and older ones to assist as well. Teenagers should definitely be doing their own laundry. Put time in your schedule to train your children to do the laundry. It will pay off in the long run. Gradually assign portions of the laundry task to them. For instance, my daughters are in the transitional stage. They have their own laundry baskets, so they fold, sort, and put away their own clothes. My son is now doing his own laundry.

Surprisingly, my girls are quite eager to graduate to doing laundry by themselves. In our home, doing the laundry is considered a grand privilege that only the mature can do. Thus we talk about it like it's a rite-of-passage exercise to prove how grown-up you really are. Some would call this brainwashing; I like to call it creative parenting.

Do not wait until your children are older to capitalize on them helping with the laundry. The best window of op-

More Household Tips

- Place containers in different rooms of your home and have your children toss in misplaced items. This provides a quick cleanup for rooms.
- Provide eye-level hooks so children can hang their own clothes up independently. They will feel good about themselves and learn responsibility early. There will also be fewer things for you to pick up.
- Color coordinate kids' cups, towels, bags, and so on so kids can be responsible for their own items. This has the added bonus of reducing sibling bickering and fosters a sense of responsibility because the kids know what items belong solely to them.

portunity is when they are toddlers and like to play with the buttons on the washing machine and dryer. (See the chart at the end of the chapter for suggested ages children may be assigned various facets of doing the laundry.) Generally I seize the opportunity and let them help, always explaining as they're assisting me that soon they will have the privilege of doing it themselves. I also have to be careful not to complain about doing the laundry in front of them lest my plan backfire.

Model correct behavior for your children at all times. We had one major flood in the basement when my son first took over the responsibility of doing his own laundry. He overstuffed the washing machine. This was indirectly my fault because he had watched me push our washing machine to its limit and warranty life on too many occasions. He reasoned, "If Mom can do it, so can I." Concerned about rising hazard-insurance fees, replacing furniture, and paying for extended warranties, I'm resolved now to always do a chore right in front of the kids and to resist taking shortcuts—especially with the laundry.

What's for Dinner?

The other area in the home that's of major concern is meal preparation. This too is a multifaceted task. It involves shopping, planning, preparing, and cooking. The time spent in this area also can be reduced.

You should only be going to the grocery store once a week or less. This can surely be accomplished with some planning. First, visit the store you frequent the most and write down the items in each aisle. Next, type up your list, if possible. Photocopy it. Write your grocery list on it; this will reduce your shopping time. You can post the paper in the kitchen, and when you notice you are low on an item, you can simply write it on the list. This will keep you from running out of items and from going to the store so frequently. It also speeds up the time you're in the store.

Write out tentative menus for a week and go shopping for these items at one time. For working moms, there are so many great cookbooks with simple meals that don't take long to prepare. Check your local library for a current listing. Take time every Saturday to plan the next week's meals. I try to plan for two weeks' worth of meals. Don't forget the kids' snacks and lunch foods. You can cook double portions and freeze the second portion. You may also cook for two weeks or even a month at a time, if you have the freezer space. Usually I purchase prepared foods when they go on sale. This helps at times.

I Can't Find the Telephone Bill

Every family should have a paper management plan. It's imperative to have a mail system because mail enters our homes on almost a daily basis. Setting up an easy mail system is simple. Get colored folders from an office supply store or Wal-Mart—they have them for only a few dollars. By the way, nearly all the department stores run sales on organizing products in January because they know one major New Year's resolution many people make is to get organized. So stock up on your organizing products then. This is also when I replace my worn folders. And yes, you will need to replace your folders yearly.

Every piece of mail should immediately be placed in one of the following folders or tossed in the trash! Label your folders as follows:

Red	To Pay—Finances
White	To Do—Now!
Yellow	To Hold—Pending
Green	To File—Later
Blue	Spouse—For Him
Orange	To Read—On the Run

Red—Your fiscal folder holds all your bills that need to be paid. A calendar should be placed inside the folder so that you can see when a particular bill is due.

White—This folder contains those things you will take immediate action on.

Yellow—This pending folder is for things to put on hold that you will eventually use but that don't need to be filed away, such as wedding invitations, directions, trash schedules, and so on.

Green—This folder is for all those items that should be filed away at a later date in your household file cabinet.

Blue—The spouse folder is for correspondence relating to your husband. Now the mail is in one uniform spot for him to read.

> Household management involves developing good habits—and remember, a habit is something you do without thinking. Good thinking forms good habits.

Orange—The reading folder is for any mail that will take over ten minutes to read.

But Mom, You Promised You Would Take Me

Another area of home management involves scheduling and time management. A family calendar is a necessity: list kids' scouting meetings, recitals, plays, trips, and so on. Put down your commitments too. Everyone should use the family calendar. You can refer to it before you make a commitment. It also helps to slow down the pace of the family a bit. You can put in the family meetings and special dinners that you want all of the family to be there for. Calendars are great!

You should also have your own personal calendar and make appointments with yourself. These appointments can be for personal development, spiritual growth, or something else. In any case, post them so family members will know you're unavailable at these times. You need to make the time to fill yourself up before you pour into others. Mothers, particularly, spend much time pouring into the lives of others but very little time filling themselves back up.

You can also reduce a lot of stress by having a family bulletin board/communication center. I have one in the kitchen. You can use a horizontal file folder or cover a cereal box with contact paper. Train your children to put any notes they receive from school or extracurricular activities in the box. This way you can read them at your leisure and not when you are cooking dinner or otherwise occupied. The communication center can also be used for encouraging notes to other family members. You can also have a suggestion box for kids and adults to write down their ideas about how the family can effectively function. A calendar should be near the family communication center.

Peace should reign in our homes as we carry the very life of God in us.

These are just a few ideas that can help you run your family more efficiently. Household management involves developing good habits—and remember, a habit is something you do without thinking. Good thinking forms good habits. We as moms set the standard for our households with our habits. It is not so important that our homes are spick-and-span clean, but that we are constantly working to improve our home-management skills to serve our families.

Nurturing an Atmosphere of Grace

Once the physical environment is in reasonable order, then we need to turn our attention to the most important aspect—the atmosphere of our home. I'm not talking about a vague esoteric concept here. Atmosphere is the real influence of your home. Atmosphere is developed by your words, your actions, and most important, your attitudes. Honestly, I do not have a full revelation of all that atmosphere involves, but I will share with you what I do know. Atmosphere is the emotional climate of an environment, and it affects people.

Upscale department stores spend a lot of money on creating an ambience or atmosphere. In addition to arranging the physical environment, various floral fragrances are used to help people feel comfortable enough to spend money there. Certain fragrances are proven to have an impact on you. This isn't surprising. Real estate agents advise home sellers to bake cakes or apple pies just before showing the

33

home so that potential buyers empathize with the home and want to buy it.

Corporations, with careful precision, create an aura about their products. Supermarkets even utilize subliminal recordings that state positive affirmations such as "I will not steal" or "I am an honest person." These messages have been proven to reduce shoplifting.

Even Jesus told his disciples when he sent them out in Matthew 10:12–13 to greet the household before they entered it and to let their peace come upon a household that was worthy. According to *Strong's Concordance*, the word *peace* there is the Greek word *eirēnē*, which means "a state of rest, quietness and calmness, an absence of strife." It denotes perfect well-being and harmonious relationships. The disciples had the ability to claim peace upon a home that was receptive to them. The atmosphere of the home beckoned a greater blessing if the occupants there received the disciples.

Peace should reign in our homes as we carry the very life of God in us. Jewish historian Josephus cites how Jesus affected people everywhere he went. We know it was God's anointing upon him. That anointing drew people to him. He was God, and the very life of God flowed from him.

Followers of Jesus likewise have the life of God in them. Peter told the lame beggar at the gate Beautiful to look upon him. The man fastened his eyes on Peter, and then he received strength in Jesus's name to walk, leap, and praise God. The beggar saw Jesus in Peter. Sick people were laid in the street, and Scripture says the very shadow of Peter healed them all. Jesus Christ alive in Peter was what healed the people. He had the very life of God living in him.

It isn't a stretch to say we too are full of the life of God and can emit peace and the presence of God in our homes. Scripture records buildings actually shaking when people prayed (Acts 16:25–26). Our homes can be havens of peace and blessings when we allow the life of God in us to affect the atmosphere.

The early church met in homes, and in fact, the environment of those homes was affected by the prayers of the people. Today we have a reverence for our churches, as we should; but we should have equal reverence for our homes. We are the temple of God (1 Cor. 6:19), and we dwell in our homes. Our homes should be called places of prayer. People in our communities ought to know where the Christian homes are. Prayer is communication with God, and that communication should be reflected in the overall atmosphere of our homes. People should be able to find refuge in those homes. The atmosphere of our homes should affect those who live there and visitors.

Hebrews 11, the great faith chapter, encourages us to have faith in God. Most of us as little children in Sunday school may have even memorized "Faith is the substance of things hoped for, the evidence of things not seen" (v. 1 KJV). This simple little verse emanates a powerful truth. The unseen realm affects us, and the greater reality is this—our homes can be affected by us believing that God wants to work in and through them. Our faith that God does indeed want to manifest his presence in our homes will affect the atmosphere of our homes, because if I believe God wants to be present in my home, that will affect everything I do and say there. Atmosphere is not just the decor of my home, but it is also summed up in my words and the attitudes I allow in my home. For instance, in my home we have a family rule that we all must speak respectfully to one another because we are all made in the image of God. When the kids are apt to bicker about something, I remind them of this truth. While I would like to say arguments never occur, I cannot. Unfortunately, disagreements often happen, but they are not the norm in our home because we try to nurture an atmosphere of peace. It is all a matter of attitude.

35

When you keep order by law, your home is regimented. When you keep order by love, your home is orderly, friendly, and very comfortable.

Strong Spiritual Homes Welcome the Presence of God

A commitment to an attitude of godliness sets the standard in the home. It is important to remember that a clean and orderly home ought to aid in your family's spiritual growth, because when things are disorderly, you are not as effective as you would like to be. A neat and orderly home must be maintained with the right attitude. You can keep order by love or by law. When you keep order by law, your home is regimented. Family members keep order out of fear of angry reprisals. Mistakes are not tolerated. There are a lot of rules and regulations to keep everyone in line, and the house is showroom perfect. Rules are made to restrict. There is a strong authoritarian spirit in this kind of home. The home is clean, yet antiseptic. In short, this home is clean, sterile, and cold!

On the other hand, when you keep order by love, your home is orderly, friendly, and very comfortable. Most things are in place, with an occasional mess here and there. The rules and regulations are there to maintain the peace. The rules are based on collective understanding and are viewed as a means of protection for everyone. Mistakes aren't met with angry reprisals but are viewed as opportunities to grow more responsible. A strong sense of team spirit is felt. This home is neat and comfortable. It is warm and endearing. There is a peace that emanates from such a home. This is the true Christian home.

Attitude is paramount in your home, because if you feel your home, children, and husband are hindering your spiritual growth, you will treat them as your enemy whether you realize it or not. Your children do not oppose a clean house nor your quiet time with the Lord; they are simply being children.

36

Children are a gift from the Lord, and anything God gives us is good. Conceptually we know this is true. Sometimes it's just that our children are not quite packaged the way we want them to be. If we're very quiet and meditative, their loudness annoys us. If we're very scholarly and our children struggle scholastically, we inwardly struggle with how to fix them. What we are really asking is how we can make them into who we want them to be. However, as different or varied as each of them is, we must accept them as our gifts.

The real issue is: what do you do with a gift? You graciously accept it. Have you ever received a strange gadget as a gift? Perhaps it was a grab bag gift or something you received at a Tupperware party. You may look at it curiously and perhaps rotate it in your hand, wondering what it is. Could it possibly have any use? Then the giver informs you that the strange gadget is a bagel splitter. Your eyes gleam, and you think about all the times you cut yourself trying to divide bagels and realize what a blessing it will be to you. Understanding brings acceptance.

As you chase after God, I want you to know that your children aren't hindering you; in fact, they are what equips you to run the race. Their innocence, their zest for life, and even their messes are molding you into a woman after God's own heart. Your insight as a mom draws you closer to the Lord. Still, there are times when you may wonder—does God really understand? How can he possibly know how I feel? This letter may express your frustrations.

I Thought You Might Want to Know, God

Dear God,

I know you're busy, but I just wanted to write to you about some of my concerns. You cannot possibly understand how it feels to be a mother.

By wisdom a house is built, and through understanding it is established; through knowledge its rooms are filled with rare and beautiful treasures.

Proverbs 24:3–4

I get no time to myself. When my kids do spend time with me, they continually ask me for something. Why can't they just enjoy my company and my presence and let me enjoy them? I have such a longing to spend personal time with them. It makes me so sad.

I tell my kids the same thing over and over and over again, yet they still do not do as I say. I'm only telling them things for their own protection. Repeating myself is so tiring, as if what I say doesn't make a difference. It is very exhausting.

Also, when I tell my kids no, they just get angry and keep asking me for the same thing even though I know it isn't good for them. I try to explain this to them, but they weary me with their constant requests. They seem to believe I am obligated to do something because they take a statement I made out of context. It is really frustrating.

When I do say yes, they never take the time to say thank you or to acknowledge my gift. Rather than expressing gratitude, they tell the other kids how good they are and brag about their gifts. Then I never see them again until they want something else. It is very disheartening.

Also, my kids bicker and magnify their differences even though I keep explaining to them that my greatest joy is to see them as one. I pray for that. Each of them seems to think I like him or her better than the others for silly, mindless reasons. I love them all with a special uncon- ditional love they cannot seem to understand. It is very discouraging.

When I'm ready to do something really great that will bless them, they move sluggishly and make excuses why it can't be done—when it is me doing all the work. When I remind them of this, they still tell me what they will do, not what I want done. It makes me very angry.

Worse yet, they tell others things I did not say. Even though they have been with me for so long, they really do not know me. Their misrepresentation of me grieves me because it causes others not to want to get to know me either.

But mainly, Lord, I am writing because I do not understand myself. Even after telling you all that they do, I just cannot bring myself to give up on them. I love them with such a special indescribable love. This love keeps driving me to believe in them, to help them grow to be all they can be. I know you probably cannot understand, Lord, but thanks for listening anyway. I just thought perhaps this letter will shed some light on how mothers really feel.

Most graciously yours,
A devoted mom

Could It Be? He Really Hears Us

Many have felt like I did when I penned this letter. In fact, anyone who engages in nurturing or growing others can identify with these feelings. I once heard someone say Jesus understood how mothers feel because he was often followed around by twelve guys who asked stupid questions and often didn't get the point. He found himself saying the same thing over and over again. Also, as you look at the unique attributes of a godly mother, you will find she mirrors the Holy Spirit. The Holy Spirit comforts, teaches, counsels, directs, and leads us into all truth.

The Holy Spirit, the third person in the Godhead, is not an elusive wind, nor an image of a dove, nor a doctrine to be clung to. Rather, he is a living, vibrant personality, and he is every bit as much God as the Father himself. His attributes of comfort, counsel, and guidance all testify to the reality to his presence.

Moms, God is with you every day, and he understands you better than you understand yourself. So continue to cry out to him for help, mercy, and strength, for he is waiting to fill you. And the great thing about God's filling is that when you get empty, he'll fill you afresh again. His Spirit is infinite.

As you pour yourself into others, he is waiting to pour himself into you. In fact, your service of ministering to the needy and the helpless is seen as a real sacrament to the Lord. For in feeding the hungry, clothing the naked, and visiting those in prison, you are directly in touch with God. Our ministry to our children, indeed the least of these, and to our husbands is seen in the heavenly realm as a great service.

As moms, much that you do will go unrecognized on this earth. But there is a book, a great book, that one day will be opened, and the Lord will thank you for changing diapers and having a good attitude with your three-year-old while she asked you a fortieth question before bedtime. Moms are really dear to the heart of God.

Receiving Our Children as Gifts

Choose to see your children as gifts to you and not weights. My three children are real gifts of the Lord to me. They are abundantly above all I could ever ask or think. I mean that sincerely! When I look at my children, I know I did not have the wisdom to ask God for them.

I so appreciate their attributes, their personalities, and the zeal with which they keep me on my toes. Perhaps in the shallowness of my soul I might have asked God for children without flaws, the kind you read about in magazines, who always clean their rooms, eat all their vegetables, and never say a sinful word. I am so glad he chose to give my children to me with their special personalities. Their lives' value cannot be measured.

Every day I see God in my children. It is my prayer that they too can daily see God in me. It is only by his mercy that I am patient, loving, kind, and long-suffering with them. I cannot do it in my own strength. I need his constant filling!

Prayer

Lord, please help me to be the kind of mom who will cause my children and my neighbors to look in my eyes and behold Jesus or step in my shadow and be healed. May my home be called a place of prayer. May my family and others find rest there.

Purposing Every Room in Your Home

Room/Space	Purpose	Activities
Nursery	Rest and sleep	Kids sleep and nap
Den	Leisure; family meeting place	Watch television, play board games, play with toys, host Little League after-game celebrations, eat snacks

Laundry Sequencing Chart

Task	Suggested Age	Ability	Able to Perform
Be aware of dirty clothes	18 months–4 years old	Fine motor beginning to develop; also emotionally able to be aware of need to pick up clothes	
Pick up clothes and put them in hamper	18 months–4 years old	Ability to grasp clothes and place them in designated place for dirty laundry	
Sort clothing (lights and darks)	3.5–6 years old	Ability to recognize colors and nuances in clothing	
Select water temperature and press appropriate buttons	2–10 years old (with parent assistance and complete supervision); 11+ (once child has been trained)	Fine motor skill to press buttons and understanding of water temperature cause/effect	
Measure detergent and put in additives when needed (bleach, fabric softener, etc.)	12+ years old (be careful—in addition to bleach fumes being toxic, detergents can be dangerous)	Ability to measure and maturity to be cautious around toxic substances. Also able to lock up detergents to keep away from younger siblings	
Time the cycle and remove clothes	12–15 years old with parental reminders; 16+ independently	Ability to plan time to return to task of completing the laundry	
Place clothes in dryer or hang dry clothes	10–15 years old with parental reminders and verbal/visual instruction; 13+ independently	Ability to follow visual and/or verbal instructions	
Sort and fold clothes	15+ years old	Ability to recognize different kinds of clothes and different family members' clothing	

3

Maintaining Your Momentum

Implementing a Realistic Schedule

After we have created an atmosphere of order and peace in our home, how do we maintain it? I've heard it said that this atmosphere is easier to obtain than it is to maintain. I am inclined to agree. The only way to do it is to manage our time. In this chapter we'll discuss some practical ways to manage our time so that we can be at peace to create an atmosphere of grace.

Not long ago, I gave my kids some parent surveys to fill out about what they felt I was or was not doing as a parent. Surprisingly, I have to admit my kids said I yell at them too much. This bothers me for two reasons. One, I hate when people yell. Overall, I am a rather reserved person and have an aversion to yelling. Two, I work very hard to cultivate an attitude of peace in our home. Yet I yell when I'm stressed for time. I may rationalize it by saying my kids choose the most inconvenient times to move slowly, although I know they're just being kids. It's hard for me to operate in that wisdom when I have my book deadline looming and clothes in the laundry basket ever multiplying while the smell of burnt lasagna is lingering in the kitchen.

Making the Right Choices

The reality of our relationship with God rests solely on the choices we make every day. Collectively, those choices become our lifestyle. And while we judge ourselves by our intentions, others judge us by our actions. I may not want to yell at my kids and may feel bad and ask God for his forgiveness, but no real change takes place until I repent.

When I repent, I say, like David did, "God, you are justified" (see Ps. 51:4). Basically, David was saying to God, "You are correct in your judgments and statutes"; and while this may seem obvious, it isn't always our attitude. We like to rationalize our sin. We must have an attitude that says, "God, your decisions are right, and I will deal with the consequences of my poor choices." As long as I am in denial, I cannot correct my behavior. After I apologize and seek God, then and only then can real change come.

Daily, we must seek God. Theologically, we understand this; but practically, it is hard to live out. By what standard do we measure whether or not a day is good? Is a day good when we are productive and can cross things off our to-do list? Or is it a good day when we have reached some magnanimous goal? Is it bad when we are frustrated and spend endless time waiting on or rocking a feverish child? Is it bad when constant interruptions affect the flow of our work? Is it bad when the house is messy, the dinner burnt, and the kids crazed? Clearly, we judge our time by our own human standards.

Those standards often relate to productivity. Tragically, many times in our quest to accomplish more, we don't

Teach us to number our days aright, that we may gain a heart of wisdom.

Psalm 90:12

realize we have removed God in the hubbub of our busy-ness. We end up doing more but feeling empty inside. This emptiness occurs when our beliefs or values—those things most important to us—and our schedules are in conflict. Many times we aren't aware of this conflict until it is too late. Sometimes as a mother I have felt the societal strain to put my baby down when I only wanted to cuddle her for a while. I knew it pleased God for me to spend time with her, but I worried about whether or not I was being productive in others' eyes.

Even the church sometimes gives us moms mixed messages. Typically, stay-at-home mothers struggle with giving too much time to church ministry as opposed to ministering to their families. Most times we do not even realize it. I once asked a time-management workshop attendee to list the things most important to her. In classic Christian style she listed (1) God, (2) husband, (3) children, (4) ministry responsibilities, and (5) job. However, to her amazement, when she tallied her time she found most of her free time was spent in church activities rather than with her husband or children.

How We Really Spend Our Time

This mom's realization forced her to make radical scheduling adjustments based on her real values. The key is to become aware of our values and plan our day so that our behaviors and beliefs fit with one another. This is a fairly simple process, but it requires brute honesty. The first step

Four Steps in Training Children

1. Let the child watch you do something.
2. Have the child participate with you.
3. Supervise the child as he or she does it.
4. Assign the task and check your child's performance.

is to list what's most important to you—your values. Write them down. Writing always brings clarity to the process. Seriously, get a notepad or your journal and answer this question: what do you value most of all?

These values are the things you really want to spend your time on. As a Christian, I have found that my values are those things God has called me to do and the lives he has called me to impact. For instance, I highly value my relationships with God, my husband, my children, and the people God has called me to impact. Yet if I get so wrapped up in serving my husband, my children, and the church, I can actually miss God. It almost sounds contradictory, but it isn't. While I place a high value on my family, I place an even higher value on God. This is easier said than done, but I have learned I can only serve my family through my service to the Lord, and therein is the balance.

Your values may be a little vague. That's all right. Now ask yourself this question: what do you think God wants you to do right now in this season of your life? The season aspect of the question is important because if you have small children, or are homeschooling, or are a missionary's wife, what God may require of you might be very different than what he would require of an empty nester.

Do you think God wants you to be more productive? Probably not in the way you think he does. I say this because we evaluate our schedules by our human standards. Most times we don't enjoy the season we are in because we're either looking to the future or looking to the past instead of enjoying the present.

Are you spending time doing those things that are important to you? Look at a typical day in your life. How much time is spent in activities that truly reflect your beliefs or values? Tally the time. Can you identify areas in your life that God may be urging you to adjust to reflect more of him? The hard part may be paring off the good to get to the best. Jesus was a master at this. He did not let people force him to do anything before the appropriate time. Over and over in Scripture, we see Jesus was not forced by the crowd to do anything. He understood his mission.

Jesus spent just three short years in public ministry, yet his impact on the world is timeless. He knew the right relationships to invest in and the right times to pray, to speak, and to be silent. His daily choices always reflected what he believed. Until our daily choices can truly reflect Christ, until what we say and what we do are the same, until our lifestyles adequately express Christ, then our Christianity will not be real to us or anyone else. We simply have to manage our time better if we want to be authentic Christians.

Balancing Our Desires and Demands

Time management is the delicate balance between our desires, the things we want to do, and the demands of our lives, the things we feel compelled to do. Typical to-do lists fail to take these important desires into account, because generally the perceived demands appear to outweigh our personal desires.

Many times we can do small, practical things to silence the demands in our lives. For instance, my husband schedules time in the evening with our children. He roughhouses with them, reviews their schoolwork, and reads stories to them. He also schedules time in his day to telephone the kids. Occasionally he takes a day off to become their substitute teacher in our home school. In this way, he balances his desire to spend time with the children with the other demands in his life.

Ask God for creative ways to balance demands and desires. We need to make sure that our desires are God-inspired desires. It is therefore necessary to stay close to his heart. This can only occur when we silence the demands that keep us away from God. The things that keep us away from God may be very subtle. For me, it was church work itself. We often find validation in church work and not in mothering. It can become very easy to confuse the two.

The time demands of the church caused me to neglect my personal time with the Lord. If anyone had asked me, I am certain I would have said, "I'm doing the Lord's work." Of course, this was just a sad excuse for poor time management. Through prayer, circumstances, and godly counsel, the Holy Spirit was able to direct me to a more balanced approach to ministry—that is, back to my first ministry, my family.

We all need a balanced approach to the demands in our lives. A close and very dear friend, a single mother, courageously took a major step to bring balance to the desires and demands in her life. She took a job with a significant decrease in her salary just so she could spend more time with her son. She often tells me she has fewer "things" but more peace. She has grown closer to God as she depends on him to meet her needs. Her relationship with her teenage son has likewise blossomed. Every time I speak with her, I am in awe and inspired, simply because she was brave enough to act on her convictions.

It takes courage to act on our convictions. It's sometimes difficult to differentiate between what we want—our desires—and what we must do. So what should we do when our desires and demands conflict? First, pray. God will give you practical solutions unique to your personal situation. Be honest. Make sure your heart is open to the adjustments God may require you to make. Also remember God has given us free will. God will speak to us, but we must choose to be obedient to what he tells us to do.

Mothering in general is devalued in our society. So when we make large investments in mothering our children, we are often made to feel as if we're oddballs or as if we're throwing our lives away. Nothing can be further from the truth. God has called us to productivity. He told Adam and Eve to be fruitful and multiply, not just in the sense of procreation, but in everything. He understands moms and their challenges to be fruitful. We need to draw close to him so he can direct our steps.

Directing our steps means leading us to places of fulfillment where our souls find rest. God gives us vision for our lives, and we become focused in our service to him and our families. Proverbs 29:18 states, "Where there is no vision, the people perish" (KJV). Moms need vision. We need to know God is with us even on our worst days when it seems everything is against us. We must draw near to God, for when we do, he will draw near to us.

What Do You Want Me to Do, Lord?

We draw near to God when we get his plan for our lives. We should have goals. Moms tend to have goals for their children, husbands, and everyone else but themselves. Our desires get circumvented so easily because we do not make goals. Stay-at-home mothers particularly need goals. Often people impose on our time because we have not set limits, so we need goals to stay focused on what God wants us to accomplish. Goal categories may include spiritual, financial, personal, professional, social, and emotional goals.

A goal without a plan is a fantasy. Every goal should have a plan with a step-by-step process for how it will be achieved. For instance, if you want to run a marathon, you will need to train. Many small steps lead up to the bigger goal of running a marathon.

Many time-management gurus talk about the importance of saying no. I have learned that it is more important to say yes. If you say yes to your goals, the things God is calling you to do, it's easier to recognize distractions and say no to them.

As my responsibilities have increased, I have learned to give a fast no and a slow yes. I generally take time before I commit to anything.

If I recognize I am called to minister creatively and yet I get a call to make brownies for my daughter's Daisy troop, I can easily say no without the guilt because I know that isn't God's plan for me. My gifting is not bent toward making brownies. Even if a volunteer is needed for the church bulletin staff, I could still say no if I was working on my goal of completing a project. On the other hand, if I get a call and feel the Holy Spirit prick my heart, I may be inclined to say yes if it's in keeping with my spiritual gifts. Generally, if something is to be added to my schedule, the Lord will deal with my heart before a request is made. Therefore, it becomes easy for me to say yes or no.

As my responsibilities have increased, I have learned to give a fast no and a slow yes. I generally take time before I commit to anything. I may seem like I make decisions slowly, but I am quite steady and am learning not to overcommit to anything that takes time from my family or God. I have had to do this because I used to be inclined to say yes instinctively, especially when I saw a pressing need. It requires great discipline on my part (as I'm sure it does on yours) not to be impulsive when I see genuine need. The

Lord is helping me not to spread myself too thin. I have to pray daily for the Lord to deliver me from jumping in and committing myself. I sometimes think I can do it all and don't realize the consequences until I have already given my word.

The Lord is helping me by teaching me to be quick to say no and prayerful when I say yes. I have the added burden of being a time-management teacher and often get very little grace when I realize I cannot keep a commitment. Therefore, I just say no so that I can say yes to God and to my family and my goals. As we take ourselves seriously, so will others.

Time Management for Moms

Time management for mothers is different than traditional time management because responding to others' needs is not generally scheduled. Frequently, we have no one to delegate to. We cannot tell our five-year-old to go start dinner. And interruptions are the norm with children. Their needs come before any to-do list, and quite frankly, they do not have any real concept of time. Standard time management does not take these factors into consideration.

Standard time management tells us to schedule tasks, listing to-do items in one of three categories: (1) must do, (2) should do, and (3) could do. Then we are told to tackle the tasks accordingly, avoiding all interruptions and delegating tasks when we're overwhelmed. None of this worked for me. First of all, everything on my list was a must do. I have no one to delegate to, and interruptions were a way of life for me. I had to be realistic.

Time management for moms begins when we take a realistic view of our time. Daily planning works best for busy mothers. Get a notebook. Make a master list of everything

Time-Management Tips for Moms

- Enjoy the moments when your children do the unpredictable.
- When planning, think through the worst-case scenario so that you are pleasantly surprised when things do go smoothly.
- Prepare as far in advance as you can (at least twenty-four hours) for family events, work, and commitments to offset last-minute surprises. There is no such thing as too much preparation.
- If you haven't done so already, invest in or make a homemade first aid kit, with bandages and medicated ointment all in one place.
- Read books on child development so you can readily respond to your children's emotional, physical, and spiritual needs.
- Always take time to think: why did this undesirable circumstance occur, and what can I do to prevent it next time?

you really need to do for the month (or, if you prefer, the next two or three months). Look at your long-term goals for guidance. Write down all the special projects in addition to the regular things you need to do each month. This is your monthly master list. I put my list in my Palm Pilot, although I handwrite it first because I still need to see it. I'm a visual person.

Record an estimated date of completion next to each item. This will help when doing your daily schedule. At this point, write down everything that comes to your mind. The sky is the limit. No filtering just yet. When you are done, leave your list alone for a while. Look at it again later. Do you still think everything on your master list is important? Your master list is where you put things you have a tendency to omit or not get to on your daily list. Write down reading a book. Be as specific as possible. While your long-term goal may be to read ten books this year, your master list should have a book that you want to read as soon as possible. In other words, the title should be listed.

Your master list should also have your housecleaning schedule and any athletic, academic, or creative arts activities your children are involved in, to the degree they affect your schedule. For example, my girls once took a dance class that required my being with them in the studio for three hours. I had to plan for those three hours, or else I would have been very exasperated. Toilet training should definitely be put on your master list. The master list may seem overwhelming, but it's the best place to sort out the things we actually are able to do.

Master lists are only as effective as the plans that piggyback off them. For instance, if you have toilet training on your list, then the question becomes, do you have a plan to toilet train? And bring this plan down to the simplest level: how will you be able to implement it? Mothers often suffer from myopic vision because we get caught up in writing the daily to-do list—which often doesn't get done. By constantly tending to the interruptions and the daily distractions, we fail to see the big picture, which makes all the difference.

Getting It All Done

The big picture is the real things of value you want to do with your children, like read the Bible to them, play a game, share a book of poetry, or go outside and play hide-and-seek. These good intentions must be put on the master list so that they can find their way to the daily to-do list. Reading the Bible through may seem like an overwhelming task, but if you make your goal just ten minutes a day, you are more apt to do it. This system isn't foolproof, but it helps us to stay anchored to what's important. You can easily lose your focus after dealing with the stomach flu for three days.

Children need a legacy of memories, not a clean house.

A master list may seem very trivial, but it helps you to do important things every day. Often it's not the amount of time spent in an activity but the consistency of the activity that counts. It's better to read your Bible every day for ten minutes than read it once a week for an hour. It becomes a habit when you are constantly doing it. Consistency builds the quality of your reading time.

Quality time is birthed through quantity time. By spending sufficient time with another, you learn about that person. You cannot have quality time unless you have a sufficient quantity of time. Our children really want us to earn it. They have a way of coming out with the most meaningful statements after they have spent time with us. Meaningful conversation builds intimacy. There is no way around it: we have to have time for our children, husbands, and other loved ones in our lives.

This brings me to an important point where time management has failed mothers. Time management experts have tried to give us succinct little schedules to follow. We do need structure, because children learn best in predictable and common settings. Emotionally, this provides them with stability. Structure establishes parameters. But scheduling our whole day restricts us and does not allow for spontaneity—a must with small children. We have to be very flexible.

Structure is like a menu with various entrées. It's a plan of action with multiple choices. For instance, I homeschool my children every day from eight o'clock in the morning to two o'clock in the afternoon. I don't do the same thing every day, but I do teach at this time. You may schedule a cleaning time but deviate from an established schedule if grape soda is all over your living room carpet. If, after

More Time-Management Tips for Moms

- Talk to mothers with children older than your children to alert you to certain developmental behaviors so your surprises will be minimal.
- When preparing for events, be sure to make a list of needed items so as not to forget anything. Prepare lists for church, shopping, and visiting grandparents. Post lists where everyone can see them.
- Take time to journal about or take pictures of some of the unpredictable joys of motherhood.
- Prepare older children for events and routines by talking to them about what you expect. (You should get fewer surprises as your children age.)
- Teach your children a few simple gestures of sign language so they can talk to you and you can respond to them when you are on the telephone. Yes and no are of course mandatory signs to know.
- Read *good* parenting magazines (not politically correct ones). Knowledge is very empowering.

you clean up the soda, you continue to clean the house, as the spill throws you off schedule, another area is bound to suffer. Limit your cleaning for that day. So am I saying forget about the laundry because you spent so much time cleaning up the soda? Of course not. Just be aware that you probably have to guard against constantly sticking with your to-do list. There will always be something to do, and when things like soda spills happen, we tend to put off spending valuable time with our children. Children need a legacy of memories, not a clean house.

Your day is structured for your protection, not to box you into unreasonable expectations. Mothers are often up late at night washing dishes and cleaning up messes just so they can start the day fresh. But tomorrow will bring more messes, spilled juice, and dirty dishes, and you will have to decide your cleanliness quotient. In pioneer days, mothers cleaned for hygienic reasons. Today, many women find their value and identity in clean homes. Is it more important to go to bed early to be able to get up for morning quiet time than to wash dirty dishes? Get paper plates. Anything that takes away too much of your time needs to be scrutinized.

Time is one entity you do not get back, and you have to manage it carefully. The Bible says we should be wise, redeeming the time. We must get the most out of our time. The Lord uses time to form our character. I am more like Jesus today than I was yesterday, and I aspire to be even more like him tomorrow. Here is a major time mistake that I've seen so many mothers make and it makes me want to cry: mothers do not take time to invest in themselves.

Fill Up So You Can Pour Out

An axiom I often use in my time-management workshops is "You get more out of your time by putting more in yourself." Christian moms, for some reason, fail to invest in themselves. I'm not sure why. I have done it myself too, but I've finally learned that an empty vessel has nothing to pour. We pour into ourselves by allowing the Lord to minister to our needs as women, wives, and mothers.

There are many practical things we can do to pour into ourselves, and these items should be put on our master to-do list. We can read good books. I suggest taking a speed-reading course, if necessary, but I have found my speed rapidly increases the more I read. Challenge yourself to read authors you don't usually read. Ask yourself if you agree or disagree with them. Read parenting books. Most moms are good about reading about parenting until their children hit six years old, when parenting resources are hard to find.

If lack of time is an issue, get audio books. Pop them in while you cook dinner or fold the laundry or wait at the soccer game. Get thought-provoking magazines or intellectually stimulating cassettes. Mars Hill Audio, for example, has an excellent audio magazine that keeps you up to snuff on what's happening around the world. Get magazines or news review services to help keep you informed. You can relay things to your children or strike up a conversation with almost anyone—and have the added benefit of having something other than the children to discuss with your husband.

When you structure your day, I'm sure you will want to break some bad habits, either yours or the kids'. Just remember, you can only work on one habit at a time. When I started working on multiple projects, I noticed I was staying up later and later. Gradually, my children began to stay up later and later. Guess what happened? You got it. They began to get out of bed later and later. Rather than trying to address their going to bed earlier—although I did, but with little consequence—I began to get them up at the crack of dawn. They naturally began to want to go to bed earlier. Of course, you realize this meant I had to go to bed earlier too.

Doing One, Two, or Three Things at the Same Time

I do not want to throw out all the traditional time-management principles. Some of them really work for us moms. Multitasking is one that I like. I try to do as many things as possible. Too much multitasking will fry your brain as you jump from thing to thing, but planned times of multitasking work great. For instance, when I'm

Still More Time-Management Tips for Moms

- Post a contingency plan for when the family may be off schedule (for example, when you have to rush to the bank, need to see a client, or cannot start dinner); that way everyone doesn't have to come to you for their marching orders.
- Post a typical family schedule where all the family can see it, so when things happen (and they always do) the whole family can see what really should have occurred.
- Get up early when you can. (I realize this is hard if you haven't gotten a good night's sleep.)
- Give kids small juice containers so they can pour their own juice. (Invest in spill-proof cups or cups with sipper seals.)
- Put things children need daily within their reach, so you are not constantly serving them.
- Assess your routines. Identify which ones still aren't working and are potential accidents waiting to happen.

cooking dinner, I usually return telephone calls, fold the laundry, clean the bathroom, and do whatever else I can do. Be careful not to overdo multitasking, as it can get you into a performance mode that will be difficult to break out of. You will find yourself always wanting to do more and more and unable to relax.

Multitasking, while effective, can cause you to be a bit flustered. I have a tendency to forget sometimes when I am doing too many things at once. Therefore, if I'm cooking dinner and I go into the schoolroom to answer a kid's question, I take the spatula with me and lay it on the desk. The spatula will remind me that I'm cooking in the kitchen. It really works. Whenever I am in one environment and go to the next, I take something from the previous environment with me. I have taken books to the bathroom, computer disks to the kitchen, laundry detergent to the

How do children spell love?

T-i-m-e.

bedroom—anything that will prominently stand out in a room. It is kind of like a game to me; it's my form of ginkgo.

Knowing whether you are a morning or a night person will also help you to plan your day. While I like staying up late, I tend to get most of my work done in the early morning; therefore, I plan my high-concentration tasks for the early morning.

Traditional time management proves delegation can work for mothers, if we give our children small tasks and follow up with them. Remember, children do not do what you expect, only what you inspect. Also, while you may not be able to delegate while your children are young, you may be able to do so when they're older. You will need to invest some teaching time in them.

Helping Our Kids Understand Time

Training children is actually quite easy and occurs in four steps. Children need to see you do something. This is the first step. You demonstrate to them how to make a bed, explaining the process as you go along. This can take place very casually. Preschoolers and toddlers naturally like to watch Mommy.

Next, have your child participate with you in making the bed. Little children also like to help Mom, so this step occurs naturally too. Let them help you smooth out the wrinkles and puff up the pillows. Be grateful and thankful for their help—letting them help you engenders a good attitude.

Then supervise your child while she makes the bed. If the child makes a mistake, go back to step two: let her make it with you. Repeat this step until she can make the bed correctly without your assistance. Step three is where most mothers fall short. We are not used to supervising. We either expect our children to know how to do something or we jump in and do it for them. Step three can be the longest in duration.

Finally, step four: assign your child the task, and occasionally check up on your child. Be certain to continue giving verbal praise and affirmation, particularly after your children have mastered a task, so they know they aren't being taken for granted. Our children need praise, approval, and attention for all the right things they do. They should also be appreciated for their contribution to the family.

The investment in training your children will pay off in the long run. Sometimes it's easier for us to just zip the child's coat rather than wait for him to do it himself. While this may seem efficient at the time, you're actually giving yourself more work as the child grows more dependent on you. Around age three or four, children insist on doing everything for themselves. Allow them. They must become autonomous, and we hurt them when we do not allow their independence.

You should communicate your schedule and expectations to your children. If your children are old enough, get organizers and planners for them. My son really wanted a Palm Pilot and has become remarkably proficient in many things since owning one. My daughter presently prefers her paper planner, but even she is making the transition. Children do not seem to have a time concept; therefore, they need to have their schedule before them. Refer to your family calendar often—it should be posted—and use a timer even when your children are doing fun things to get them to have an understanding of time.

Children spell love t-i-m-e; therefore, it behooves you to give them time. Sometimes we can be there but not be there, if you know what I mean. We can be physically present but have a million things on our minds. Even stay-at-home mothers have to guard against finding their identity in mothers' groups, church service, or anything outside of Christ Jesus himself.

I have been guilty of spending too much time handling other people's problems. The Lord showed me I was giving away my children's inheritance when others were allowed to take me from them. I should counsel others, pray for them, and in that way be there for them, but never to the detriment of my family. It isn't wrong to help other people, but often we are finding our identity in groups, albeit Christian groups. These good things keep us from God's best. I am not saying not to serve others. We should, but not at the expense of our families.

Moms should try to spend time with their children individually as much as possible. Mothers with many children will think this impossible. It is not. Make it a priority. Put it on your master to-do list, and then schedule time for it. Children need concentrated chunks of time when you focus just on them. My son likes to cook with me sometimes. My daughter and I share a few words from a book. My youngest still sits in my lap, and we ask each other silly questions. Children need to be talked to, touched, and tapped into every day. Ask them what they think; and remember, it takes time for them to get to the real issue, so be ready to give them lots of quantity time every day if you want quality time in return.

A Realistic To-Do List

Once we have made our master list and included time for our children, we must make a daily schedule. Generally, we are told to plan our day from morning to night; but the Lord shows us a better way. In Genesis, we learn that the evening and the morning were the first day. Thus, we should plan "backward." This was an essential paradigm shift for me: start at the end and work to the beginning.

It's actually quite easy. I think about how I want my day to begin. When I look at my master list, I see one of my goals is to have time alone with God in the morning. In order to have quiet time in the morning, I have to get up early. Well, that means I have to go to bed early; and that means the kids have to go to bed even earlier. That means they have to take baths by seven o'clock, which means they have to eat dinner by six o'clock. So I can see the key to having my quiet time is really serving dinner at six o'clock. It helps to think like this, because if we think linearly, we might miss the nuances that really disrupt our schedule. Try it.

Moms, especially moms with small children, typically try to cram too much into a day. They often frustrate themselves by demanding the impossible. These mothers spend naptime running around doing more instead of using it for rest or refreshment. Sometimes we're programmed to believe our worth is in what we do, and we find it hard to slow down.

Notwithstanding the tendency to do too much, every mom needs a schedule. Your schedule shouldn't be so rigid that it does not allow room to alter it. Some moms are so perfectionist that they create a schedule God himself cannot interrupt.

Gain perspective on what a reasonable schedule would be for your family by creating a perfect-day schedule. Once you make this schedule, prayerfully ask God to make your expectations realistic. Seriously, take the schedule to God and then do an alternative schedule with God's insight and your desires. I know this sounds a bit weird, but God wants to speak to us in all the details of our day.

You are more productive when you are at peace; and you cannot have peace if you are not at peace. Guard your peace by writing things down in your daily calendar. A monthly at-a-glance calendar is a necessity for a busy family. By writing things down, you free your mind to think on other things.

Exercise. I find I'm more energetic when I do. Start in small increments—even running in the backyard with your kids is exercise.

Use all available time. Sometimes we think we don't have time, when what we really mean is we only have small increments of time. We may not get an hour to pray, but we can pray for ten minutes. Minutes add up to hours. You may never find three hours to clean the garage, but you can begin working on it ten minutes a day instead of endlessly procrastinating because you do not have a large chunk of time.

Living with Jesus

Truly, all our time is God's time. Jesus stepped into time and taught us how to live our finite lives in infinite proportions. He taught his followers in his everyday life. They noticed what Jesus said in the multitudes and how he lived in the ordinary. They watched him stop to play with children. They saw the compassion in his eyes when he healed a blind man. They saw the love in his words when he affirmed the woman with the issue of blood. The disciples watched how he made decisions, treated others, and just did ordinary things. Jesus was a man of confluence. The disciples saw by his life that he actually believed what he said. In other words, Jesus never made a decision in a moment of time; it was already rooted in his character. We too make decisions every day in the ordinary activities of our day. It would be such a blessing to our children, our husbands, and all those we encounter if we could just have the character of Jesus reflected in our day-to-day activities.

As Christian moms, what we say and do must reflect who Christ is, because he lives in us. Others must behold him in us. I make this statement not to condemn us, because life happens to all of us and none of us is perfect. The great thing about God is that he never requires us to do something that we are incapable of doing. We simply ask for his help. We are always on God's mind. The issue for us is to have the presence of mind to think of God, for he is always thinking of us. In the next chapter, we will talk about how we can keep our minds on Jesus.

Prayer

Lord, I give my time to you. Help me to give it to you wholly. Use it for your glory.

4

As a Mother Thinketh, So Is She

Having Peaceful, Practical, and Productive Thoughts

After we have gotten our home and time in order, we have to tackle the hardest part: getting our minds in order. Proverbs 23:7 informs us that "as [a man] thinketh in his heart, so is he" (KJV). Psychologists and counselors all agree that when we change our perception, we change our world, because what we do and see is framed by what we believe. Our beliefs form our lifestyle. Mothers typically get so busy that they are not aware of their thoughts. This is not good.

It has been said that Satan delights in noise, hurry, and crowds. Can you think of any better words to describe a home with a busy toddler? It's usually full of noise, hurry, and the relentless, incessant demands of a two-year-old—which often seem like the demands of a whole crowd. Overall, our society is full of busyness, loudness, and superficiality. We carry planners, organizers, cell phones, and beepers, afraid we might miss something.

The story is told of some missionaries and their African guides who had a powerful evangelistic meeting that lasted until the wee hours of the morning. The American missionaries rose early the next morning, tired but convinced they had to continue on with their journey. They found their African guides fast asleep. When they inquired of the guides how they could sleep after such an anointed meeting, the guides reasoned, "We need time for our bodies to catch up with our souls."

When you have too much on your mind or the wrong things on your mind, it doesn't operate at peak performance.

It isn't just mothers who need to find a quiet moment these days; all of us suffer to some degree from the lack of quiet in our lives. We find it difficult to be still. Stillness makes our generation uncomfortable because it causes us to think. The people of this generation have been characterized as non-thinkers. We accept anything and are enmeshed in achieving more, but many of our lives lack substance. Yet God says, "Be still, and know that I am God" (Ps. 46:10).

Resting in God is hard for us. Each time we add something to our schedule, we engage our minds. As a result, our minds are constantly racing. Some mothers lie down and get back up tired because their minds are so occupied by everything they have to do. There have been times when I had so much on my mind that I could not remember exactly what I had to do at a particular moment. The mind is quite complex, and it's difficult to determine all the nuances of your mind. Suffice it to say, when you have too much on your mind or the wrong things on your mind, it doesn't operate at peak performance.

Learning to Think Like God

God's ability is awesome. He holds the world together by the power of his will and his words, and yet he can

Meditation makes God's Word a reality to us. take the time to listen to us. Obviously, he does not get overwhelmed. One thing is certain: we do not always think like God. Isaiah 55:8 declares, "My thoughts are not your thoughts, nor are your ways my ways" (NKJV). Inherent in this verse is the idea that as we learn about God's thoughts and ways, we can begin to make better decisions and learn to become more like him. There is only one way to understand God's thoughts: we must meditate on his Word.

Meditation makes God's Word a reality to us. Meditation is a lost biblical practice in the modern church. Our spiritual forefathers—Martin Luther, Brother Lawrence, Jonathan Edwards—all regularly meditated. Meditation was a regular part of the lives of biblical characters Isaac, Joshua, and David. Scripture is full of directives to meditate on the Word of God.

Biblical meditation is not to be confused with transcendental meditation, which involves chanting and emptying your mind. God didn't design your mind to be empty; therefore, the practice of transcendental meditation has other origins. If your mind is not filled with God, it must be opened up to Satan's influences.

Biblical meditation fills your mind with the Word of God. Its benefits are immense. It makes the Word of God real because the Word is personalized and internalized. We have a scriptural mandate to meditate and the promise that we will prosper if we do (Psalm 1). Most importantly, meditation helps us to think like God.

This spiritual discipline will yield tremendous results and requires very little time and effort to initiate. Little things like daily meditation yield large lifetime benefits. Sometimes busy mothers do not need more time; rather, we need to be efficient in the use of the small segments of free time we do have. Meditation, or pondering over Scripture,

Ways to Remember Scripture

- Use pictures with figures or symbols to trigger words you need to remember.
- Use music—turn Scriptures into songs. Use well-known songs or create your own. (Many people have learned the books of the Bible by memorizing them to the tune of "Row, Row, Row Your Boat.")
- Use movement and hand gestures.
- Write or type the Scripture over and over.

can be done in little increments. Scripture is living and vibrant and, taken in even small doses, yields large returns. In the truest sense of meditating on Scripture, we begin to think like God. Imagine that!

Meditation is different from Bible reading or Bible study in that it is slow and contemplative. It is experiencing God in his written Word as we slowly ponder each word. It is the slow, reflective process that makes meditation so effective. Therefore, choose very small segments of Scripture, perhaps one Bible verse. Committing to ten or fifteen minutes tops is a good way to begin meditation.

The context of Scripture is important, and while meditation is not Bible study, you should thoroughly read the full scope of the verse you are meditating on, including the verses before and after it. Be aware of the historic context, who the Scripture was written to, and why the Scripture may have been written. Context is crucial. Remember, the devil took Scripture out of context and used it to tempt Jesus.

Jesus was able to stand against the temptation because he knew the Word in context. Context grants us understanding. Likewise, we can only stand against Satan to the degree we have an understanding of Scripture.

Proverbs and Psalms are excellent books to meditate on because they contain compact, singular themes and

Basic Meditation Principles

- Read Scripture slowly and reverently. Reread it many times.
- Study Scripture. Read it in context.
- Use study aids sparingly. Do not rely on them, but use them as a guide.
- Write out the Scripture.
- Ask yourself what the Scripture means to you personally, right where you are at this present time.
- Accept the Scripture as God's Word to you right now.
- Ask if the Lord is affirming you or challenging you to change in a certain area.
- Confess your sin or shortcoming.
- Repent. Do not make excuses for your sin.
- Ask God for the grace to change. Resolve to be committed to God working out his plan in your life.
- Pray the Scripture, inserting your name if it's appropriate, especially if the Scripture contains a blessing, a promise, a plead, or a prayer.
- Ask if the Scripture gives you insight into how you can change, and obey its directive immediately.
- Become a doer of the Word. Obey God's Word.
- Commit to a consistent time to refresh yourself in God's presence.

thoughts; therefore, it's easy to understand context. The Proverbs have many practical verses, while the Psalms contain praise, worship, and theological references. But don't limit yourself to just Psalms or Proverbs. New Testament Scripture is rich with revelation, especially the words of Jesus.

Prayerfully choose Scripture. If you are interested in a theme such as love or forgiveness, use your concordance to locate relevant Scriptures to meditate on. If you are challenged with a loose tongue, meditate on Scriptures about controlling the tongue. Meditation is seeing the Scripture's meaning and practical application. Effective meditation always results in a changed lifestyle or obedience to God's Word.

You simply must engender a personal investment in meditation for it to be effective, or else you will give up on it when hard times come to challenge your consistency. You are more apt to persist in something when you can see the fruits of your labor. Therefore, rather than just choosing a Scripture at random, pick one that really means something to you.

Once you have chosen a Scripture, sit in a quiet spot and read it slowly. Ask God to open your understanding of the verse. In Luke 24:45, Jesus, after his resurrection, opens up the disciples' understanding of Scripture. We have the privilege to ask the same of him. In fact, we need him to illuminate our understanding of the Word. As we read slowly and contemplatively, we may ask the Holy Spirit questions.

We must eagerly and patiently wait for the answers. Guard against answering your own questions. Give time for the Lord to speak to your heart. Sometimes you won't get the answer to an inquiry immediately. God is not a magic man of tricks whom we can turn off and on at will. Specifically, we see in Scripture that there were often time lapses between a prayer's request and God's response or answer. After all, Daniel waited twenty-one days for a response (Dan. 10:13).

Genuinely inquire about elements of the Scripture you may not understand, because meditation is interactive. God actually participates with us as we reflect on his Word. We must read reflectively, asking questions all the time. We question to keep our minds actively engaged, just as we would when we read our Bibles.

We must likewise read prayerfully and expectantly, asking the Lord to show us his will. Be careful—it is God's will that all of us are conformed to the image of his Son, Jesus, and so we can and should expect God to speak to us about character issues during our meditation.

Meditation is a spiritual discipline, and we must rest in the assurance that God will teach us what we need to know when we need to know it. Likewise, we must have a teachable attitude to welcome the Holy Spirit into the process.

Meditation really personalizes Scripture; therefore, it is imperative we keep track as we engage in this spiritual discipline. Document your meditation times. Get a special journal. Some biblical scholars believed strongly in the practice of writing out the Scriptures they were meditating on. Thus they were known to sit down and manually write down Scripture repeatedly on an almost daily basis. I'm not sure what they would think of computers, as they relished the process of handwriting Scripture, which was thought to be divine. Actually, I still prefer writing it down. Writing Scripture commits us to daily meditation in a tangible way.

Meditation is not a typical "one, two, three, you do this" spiritual discipline. It does operate under basic principles, but not in a prescribed order. The major principle of meditation is repetition. You read the Scripture, reflecting on its historical and biblical context. You then observe what it says. Look at the Scripture. Read it slowly a few times. Pray. Ask: What does it mean? How might the verse be interpreted? What does the verse mean to me? Once these questions are answered—and they might not all be answered in one sitting—persist in moving on to another portion of Scripture that may be confusing to you. Trust the Lord to illuminate the Scripture to you. Once you feel sufficiently enlightened on one verse, move on to the next.

Wait upon God patiently and expectantly. This is perhaps the most important part of the meditation process.

Meditation Helps

- An orderly environment. A clean home helps us to concentrate because our minds crave order.
- Instrumental worship music. Soft, instrumental music is relaxing and calming and helps us to focus on the Lord.
- Solitude. Take a walk if necessary. Being alone and out in nature helps us to focus on just us and God.
- Exercise. Jogging or other exercise actually gets blood flowing to the brain and helps us think clearly. Many people report that their most special time with the Lord is through prayer walking.
- Weekend retreats. Occasionally go on a contemplative retreat. Your children and spouse can accompany you as long as everyone's goal is to seek God.

Slow, quiet, and uninterrupted time is best for meditation, because we must wait for revelation. When you first begin, you may only be able to meditate for very brief periods, perhaps even less than five minutes. This is fine.

The key is consistency. Ask God to help you to be faithful. Come to him with resolve, and watch him open up the Scriptures to you. I must stress the repetitive process of meditation, because our minds are prone to wander. We must force ourselves to come back to the Scripture at hand. When our mind wanders, we can say no to the idle thought and repeat the Scripture. By doing this, we exercise our minds to be strong and purposeful.

The final principle of meditation is that the Word must be applied to our lives. This is the hardest but the most effective part of the process. Our meditation must be purposeful and must change our life. Application is what makes the difference. It represents the transformation process at its best. Meditation should change you. It is not to be applied to others, except to the degree that their actions reflect on you. We must have a teachable attitude as we approach meditation, because we are receiving God's thoughts. Therefore, we have to relinquish our thoughts. We should pray before we meditate that we have the courage, strength, and determination to change those things in our character that God directs us to change.

As you repeat the Scripture over and over, asking God to show you what it means for your life, be ready for him to point out the sin and the good that keep us from his best. Answer the Lord, and be willing to surrender when he directs you to change your thinking or your attitude. You are engaged in building a relationship with your Creator, and God is concerned about quality, not quantity, so do not rush things. Listen and respond. This relationship is developed in these interactions. The practice of meditation readies our hearts to hear him throughout the day.

There are other things you can do to enrich your meditation time. Some people like to have soft music in the background as they meditate; others like to hear nature sounds. Still others prefer total silence.

As you ponder over a Scripture, personalize it. When you read in Psalm 23, "The Lord is my shepherd," say it as if the Lord is your shepherd. When you read in Psalm 1, "Blessed is the man who walks not in the counsel of the ungodly" (NKJV), replace the word *man* with your name. Say, "Blessed is Cheryl, since I walk not in the counsel of the ungodly." Then pray, "Lord, help me not to walk in the counsel of the ungodly."

Memorizing helps in the application process, and memorization assures God will be able to bring the verse to your remembrance sometime in the future. Meditation should be coupled with Bible study, because we should wash our minds with the water of the Word. This should be done daily.

Can I Really Do This?

But how can I read my Bible and meditate on Scripture every day? Often we just think of the traditional way of sitting down and reading. Busy moms rarely have long stretches of time to do anything, especially read the Bible. There are other ways to read and meditate. It just requires some creativity. The most important thing is to place Bible verses where we can easily see them. We should try to keep them before our eyes.

Posting Scripture everywhere you are likely to look is an effective means of keeping it before your eyes. Deuteronomy 6:6–9 states, "These commandments that I give you today are to be upon your hearts. Impress them on your children. Talk about them when you sit at home and when you walk along the road, when you lie down and when you get up. Tie them as symbols on your hands and bind them on your foreheads. Write them on the doorframes of your houses and on your gates." This Scripture lets us know that Scripture should be a natural part of our lives.

Some Orthodox Jews take this Scripture literally and actually carry Scripture on them, making it part of their clothing. This concept may be altered a bit: we may write Scripture on index cards and carry them around with us. Rather than choosing Scripture at random, choose Scripture that you want to transform your mind. Remember, we discussed choosing Scripture themes that mean something to you. This is most important when carrying Scripture around. For example, if you're struggling with depression, then Scriptures on the joy of the Lord are appropriate. You can pull out a card and meditate on it when a depressing thought comes. This gets the Word in your heart.

Most importantly, the Word should be in our hearts; but first, it should be everywhere else, because before we can get it in our hearts, we must see it with our eyes. Posting

> Do not conform any longer to the pattern of this world, but be transformed by the renewing of your mind. Then you will be able to test and approve what God's will is—his good, pleasing and perfect will.
>
> Romans 12:2

Scripture prominently in our homes assists us with biblical meditation because it does not require scheduled quiet. You may meditate whenever you get a few moments. While I would agree that quiet moments are rare, they certainly do occur, often without our foreknowledge. Having Scripture before you capitalizes on those moments. Suppose the kids suddenly play together quietly for ten minutes in the living room. You can turn to a hanging scriptural plaque and meditate on the Scripture while they play nearby.

It's all about making meditation a priority. Some mothers do not meditate because they think they don't have the time. What they really mean is that they don't have a huge, ideal block of time to sit and read uninterrupted. Such luxuries are limited for mothers; therefore, we have to make the written Word become part of our everyday activities.

This can be done easily and in creative and economical ways. Computers and art stores make it very easy for us to make printed Scripture have visual appeal. There are many ideas with a negligible cost. You may print Scripture on colored party or theme paper, available from an office supply store. Be sure to type the Scripture in a large font that is easy to read.

Be creative: Post Scripture in your child's room and play area. Use old calendars with nature scenes and type Scripture underneath the picture. Frame the picture. Scenic pictures can be placed in the bathroom and hallway. As we look on them, we'll be reminded to meditate on the Scripture on them. If your handwriting is legible, write the Scripture yourself, as handwritten Scriptures may be put in private places where it's easier to change the Scripture without a lot of fanfare. Sticky pads are excellent for posting Scripture in the bathroom.

Jesus did not say the truth will make you free. He said the truth you *know* will set you free.

Remember to post some Scripture at your child's eye level. Use magazine pictures. For example, if you wanted your child to memorize "My sheep listen to my voice" (John 10:27), you could cut out a picture of a sheep and glue it on the Scripture poster. You may also have your child draw a picture and add a Scripture to it. Frame the drawing. That will mean a lot to your child and may even make the Scripture a favorite. Hang the picture in a prominent place in your home.

Post Scripture in the bathroom, kitchen, foyer, living room closet—almost anyplace. Since you have determined the purpose of each room in your house from chapter 2, consider posting Scripture relevant to the purpose. If you have a television set in your den, you might post Proverbs 27:12: "A prudent man foreseeth the evil, and hideth himself; but the simple pass on, and are punished" (KJV). This encourages everyone to meditate on the Scripture and may discourage inappropriate television viewing. Impress upon family members that they can avoid evil by not watching certain television shows.

There are other ways to keep Scripture before your eyes. I do not want to neglect the obvious, which is to buy Christian art. In fact, some of the best art in our home was done by Christian artists. Purchasing plaques at a Christian variety store or bookstore or adding Scripture verses to regular art are also options. You may also bring into your home elements of nature that remind you of God. I find this especially effective through the winter months. Elements that are foreign to your home foster an appreciation of God's

More Meditation Helps

- Have an uninterrupted day you dedicate to prayer. You may schedule a day at home dedicated just to the Lord. Put aside your usual routine and focus on him. Include your children or just schedule small chunks of time.
- Get a babysitter and spend time with just you and the Lord. There is no better investment of your time and efforts.
- Use naptime as your meditation time. The house will be very quiet.
- Be out in nature as much as possible when meditating. Sit on your back porch or visit a neighborhood park. The natural elements can be very calming. More importantly, being in nature really separates us from the hustle and bustle of our busy technological lives.
- Ask yourself who, what, why, when, and how so that the Scripture becomes clear to you when meditating. Asking questions keeps your mind active. Remember, biblical meditation encourages you to use your mind, not empty it, so keeping it engaged is important.

creation. Seashells, rocks, and plants are just a few things that can be made into a display of God's goodness. I have collections and post Scripture with each collection.

Obviously, the possibilities are endless. Post Scripture in your car, right on the steering wheel, or on your computer screen saver. You may also memorize whole books of the Bible by getting miniature books with Scripture in them. I am working on memorizing the book of James with the help of *Scripture Memory Aids*. This book is out of print, but you can simply copy portions of Scripture on your computer and organize them into clusters so you merely have to memorize the clusters. It is less intimidating than memorizing a whole book. I like to enlarge the print as well because it helps me to get a real picture of the passage. It keeps my mind active and alert. If we fill our thoughts with God, we have something to draw on from our reservoirs. See the lists earlier in this chapter for various meditation helps.

Change Scripture weekly, monthly, or quarterly, whichever is best for you. I like to leave it posted for a while to ensure my children internalize the Scripture. It has been said that the best way to show we know something is to teach others. Our children are our best students. If you can teach what you have meditated on to your children with practical application, then it truly has transformed you. The posted Scriptures will not change you. Jesus did not say the truth will make you free. He said the truth you *know* will set you free (John 8:32).

Knowing Scripture takes time. Once the Scripture is posted, you will have to consciously and deliberately reflect on it. Read it slowly over and over again, asking God and yourself what it really means. Memorize it. Think of ways you can practically apply the verse. Determine to apply the verse that day. Repent immediately. Do not fall into the trap of convincing yourself you will repent to the Lord when you have time alone with him. Be quick to repent as soon as you get the revelation. Pray the Scripture back to God. Truly let the Scripture transform you.

Invite your children in on the process. While toddlers will not fully understand the process of meditation, they do understand "Let's pray!" You can teach children to look at Scripture and to memorize it and apply it by giving them an opportunity to teach one another or a "class" of stuffed animals or dolls.

Using All Our Senses to Help Us

Besides putting Scripture before your eyes, you can engage all your senses. You may have potpourri throughout

When we want to change how we feel about something, we have to change what we do and say.

the house to represent the fragrance of the Lord. Fragrant oils may be used. Bath oils and accompanying worshipful music can put you in a meditative mood. Praise and worship hymns can be played throughout the day. Use different songs as prayers to the Lord. One of my favorite songs is "I'll Trust You, Lord," by Donnie McClurkin. I sing it as a prayer to the Lord. I make a conscious effort to stop during the day to listen to the words of the song. It is my prayer of supplication that I will trust him more and more. Guard your mind by listening to anointed music.

The Word of God is so powerful, and hearing it is transforming. As a young mom, I often used the Bible on cassette because I was so tired I would fall asleep while reading the Bible. I like the dramatized version because my kids will listen to it with me, and it actually engaged me on nights when I was really tired. I have also played the Bible tapes while I drifted off to sleep. Check to make sure they do not keep your husband up.

We have often had our children drift off to sleep listening to the Bible or worshipful music. Be careful what Bible stories you choose for your children to listen to. Once our children were listening to the cassettes and were frightened by the dramatic effects of Satan's voice. That was the only time it backfired; now we just let their souls feast on Scriptures of comfort and confidence. During cold and flu season, we had them listening to healing Scriptures set to melodic music.

Children need to engage their senses to learn, and music is a necessary ingredient in their spiritual development. Small children can play with praise and worship songs playing softly in the background. This music has an almost subliminal effect on them. Subliminal need not be a negative thing. In this case, children will begin to sing praise music and to memorize Scripture almost effortlessly. There are also innumerable recordings of Christian children's music, much of it biblically based. In fact, the video *NIV Kids Club 2000* has three exceptionally cute kids in it. (Read the credits and you'll see the names of the Carter kids.) Just do what comes to you instinctively as a mom. When my children were preschoolers, I would pick them up and pray and sing with them in my arms, and my children have learned to enjoy praise and worship music.

Make cookies or another food with your child and offer that time up to the Lord in prayer. You might celebrate Passover by making matzo balls. You can make food to commemorate certain holidays and to pray for different cultures. The key is to keep the Lord ever present in your mind in whatever you do. Meditation is the best source of spiritual strength.

Not Going Out of Our Minds

A purposeful mind is a mind that keeps thoughts in order. It controls idle thoughts. In fact, Christian counselors usually recommend meditating on who you are in Christ when dealing with almost any syndrome.

Our thoughts and behaviors are so cyclical that it's difficult to determine which originated first, the thought or the feeling. We know that thoughts of hopelessness and helplessness produce depression. Yet at the same time, we know that once we have achieved something, it empowers us to do even more.

It's interesting—when we want to change how we feel about something, we have to change what we do and say. For instance, if we want to endear someone to us, we hug the person. It's been proven that if you hug the person long enough,

Thinking about things you can do nothing about is a waste of time.

you begin to have thoughts of fondness toward him or her. It has also been proven that if you keep telling yourself you love someone, eventually you will grow fond of the person. I'm not sure we have a full understanding of which came first, the chicken or the egg.

Suffice it to say that as mothers we can engage our thoughts and actions at the same time to keep us away from negative and unhealthy thinking. Sometimes we have to do something to elicit an emotion. Purposeful thinking is a necessity for mothers, because we're often plagued by negative thinking that produces negative feelings. Yet these negative feelings are merely the result of a mother's own negative thoughts. Negative feelings reinforce negative behavior, and so the cycle continues.

I have seen too many mothers slip into the abyss simply because they did not control their minds. Negative thoughts consume us at times. This is not necessarily demonic; by nature, we are negative. Sometimes the worst scenarios come to mind. We have also seen our mothers worry, and we pattern our behavior accordingly.

Worry is fear, and both come from many places. The media feeds on our fear and magnifies it. We have so many negative thoughts rooted in insecurity and uncertainty. Thoughts come so fast and furious that we hardly recognize what is going on. Proverbs 4:23 says, "Guard your heart, for it is the wellspring of life."

Our minds really require a constant cleansing in the Word of God. Only Scripture can remove the debris. It requires diligence on our part. We must make a decision to have a strong mind and to take every thought captive to the obedience of Christ. Our minds are like a field, and thoughts are merely seeds. We decide which seeds will grow.

We can determine which thoughts we will harvest. Remember, once you meditate on a thought, it eventually becomes a feeling. The feeling is more intense the more time we spend meditating on a thought. This is not an iron-clad rule, but generally, all our actions are a result of our feelings. If we get a thought that is clearly not from God, we must refuse it. We know a thought is not from God if it isn't good, true, and lovely (Phil. 4:8 KJV). It should have virtue and praise and should bring you closer to God. If the thought doesn't bring you closer to God, refuse it; reject it. Say out loud, "I refuse you in the name of Jesus." Keep doing this, even if the negative thought comes back again. Do not think about it. Meditating on God's Word works in the positive, inviting God in; likewise, meditating on problems and circumstances will invite the enemy in.

As you continually resist a thought, it will go away. You water the seeds of your thoughts by pondering them. Eventually a thought will stop returning as your thinking becomes more purposeful.

Be sure you aren't refuting a thought from the throne by asking yourself what would be the fruit of the seed of that thought. For instance, if your son is out late and you hear about a fire, and you get a thought that he is in the fire, does that thought bring joy? No, it does not. The Lord would direct you to pray or give you peace, in the midst of your worrying, that your son isn't in the fire. It has been said that worrying is a substitute for prayer. When we are tempted to worry, we must turn to prayerful meditation to keep wrong thoughts away from us.

Sometimes wrong thoughts are not inherently evil, but they keep us from coming up higher in God. Often the Lord may direct us to give up something good to get something better. Many times God has directed my thoughts in areas that really surprised me. For instance, the Lord once impressed upon me to be authentic in my communication, not just in my words, but in my thoughts toward others. In other words, I shouldn't just wish someone well but be

Hindrances to Effective Biblical Meditation

- Judging the Word instead of reading and applying it. We assume we know what all Scripture means because we have heard it all before; therefore, we don't expect to get something out of our meditation time.
- Listening to what others have told us Scripture means rather than reading it for ourselves.
- Having wrong priorities and not understanding the importance of this spiritual discipline in our Christian growth.
- Expecting instant results. Meditation is a slow process and yields the most results when done consistently. Those who choose a lifestyle of meditation will receive the most results.
- Having a worldly mind-set. Meditation requires quietness and stillness. We must stop our pursuit of money and rush of activity. At times, we may unconsciously value the world's way over time alone with God, because spending time with God requires faith and trust. While we may trust God, we may not trust ourselves to really glean from the meditation process.

genuinely excited when someone receives a blessing I am still praying to acquire.

Our thought life can become loftier if we consecrate it to God. Meditation opens the door for this kind of communication. We all know not to gossip or to take joy when someone who has wronged us gets punished. Those things are obvious. It's the little foxes that ensnare us at times. Keeping Scripture ever present in our hearts really fosters Christian maturity. It keeps us thinking on things that are true, lovely, and of good report.

We waste a lot of time meditating on other people's problems that we aren't called to fix. In my time-management workshops, I tell the women that thinking about things you can do nothing about is a waste of time. Once I was tutoring a student who had a very bad attitude. I knew the student's parents, and his home life seemed rather stable. I wondered too much about how this young man had become so cynical and negative about everything. The Lord nudged me that it was not my concern. I was to pray and to teach him, and he was doing very well in tutoring. I was not called to solve his family's problems and was wasting my valuable time with suppositions and innuendoes about the family. When we think on things we should not, we're in danger of falling into the sin of judgment.

Check the things you are thinking about, and then ask God if you are called to be thinking about them. If not, then immediately replace them with what you should be thinking about. I have found replacing thoughts to be easy for me. Once my husband and I were having an argument, and I got a letter in the mail confirming an event we both wanted to attend. Quickly we realized how petty our disagreement had been as we excitedly discussed our impending trip. Sometimes our thoughts are too low when we are consumed by ourselves and engaged in self-pity, pride, or anger.

It's a matter of consecration as we ask God to take our good and make it his best. You can come up higher in your thinking by choosing to meditate on Scripture and diligently seeking God's opinion on everything. Replacing our thoughts with the Word of God is very powerful. For instance, rather than meditating on the wrong action of a friend, I can meditate on forgiveness. This will affect how I react to my friend and yield a godly instead of a vengeful response when I see her.

Sometimes, despite our best efforts, we won't be able to discern if our thoughts are good seeds that we should water and allow to grow or impure seeds that we need to yank out before they take root. We know thoughts of guilt, shame, and distress are evil reports or seeds we should

But his delight is in the law of the Lord, and on his law he meditates day and night.

Psalm 1:2

not receive. If we allow these negative thoughts to sprout, they will yield negative emotions and eventually negative behaviors.

If a negative thought comes to you, take it to God first. Discern what will be the fruit of you meditating on that thought. Is there a portion of Scripture that refutes the thought? Is it a thought that would please God? Is it there to edify you or to draw you closer to God? Check with other godly counselors before you accept the thought, especially if it causes you to feel uneasy. Remember, not all negative thoughts are satanically inspired. Sometimes we are just too negative and tend to think the worst. That's why there is safety in a multitude of counselors. Our pastors, teachers, and others are there to help us hear from God. Above all, the Holy Spirit is our counselor, and he will guide us in the process.

Speak, Lord, I Hear You

Finally, if God speaks to us, we must act immediately. When God speaks, he expects immediate action. Even if he speaks to you in the morning and tells you to have a good attitude when your husband returns from work in the evening, it is at that moment your attitude must change, not in the evening when your husband comes home. God speaks in the immediate. God's thoughts embrace peace. His rebukes emanate love and promise hope when you obediently heed his words.

Meditation may be defined as "thinking God's thoughts with him." Thoughts may come to us from the things we're exposed to in our environment: the television shows we watch, the people we talk to, the music we listen to, or anything in the sensory realm. Our subconscious mind also gives us thoughts. These are hard to detect because they are usually vague, under-the-surface thoughts. They were formed in our childhood and through various experiences. Last, thoughts may come from the spirit realm—either God or Satan.

We must understand that we see through a glass, darkly. No matter what our minds are thinking, God sees the whole picture. God has promised to lead us into all truth, and he alone sees clearly (John 16:13). Our sensory processes are incapable of perceiving things the way God wants us to see them. We must therefore turn to God and ask him to help us see the truth. Next comes the hard part. We must stop our way of thinking and listen for God's truth. We ask him to help us see the reality beyond the appearance. We must then respond to God's revelation. We must continually practice purposeful thinking.

We must try not to reason using our own thought processes. We know that God loves us and that his Spirit lives in us. He wants us to come to him. As we set our hearts and minds to listen to him, we will hear his voice in our everyday activities. Most of us recognize our dependence on God, yet few of us know we still must submit to him on a moment-by-moment basis. We must guard the things we put in our minds. Our minds are the primary tool God uses to speak to us, and we must be faithful in stewarding our minds properly.

Scriptural meditation is important and can change our minds. This process can be solidified in our quiet time. This is our greatest challenge: to have a regular quiet time. We will discuss some practical ways to have a consistent quiet time in the next chapter.

Prayer

Lord, I give my mind to you. Use it for your glory. Help me to think on those things that are lovely, just, and of a good report.

5

Is It Really Possible?

How to *Really* Have a Consistent Quiet Time

Quiet time is a necessity for moms for so many reasons. Mainly it is where we get filled up so we can give out. It secures us emotionally. Let's face it, motherhood can be emotionally draining. We have to be patient with whining children, busy husbands, and a relentless to-do list; and our strength is drawn from quiet time. Quiet time also develops us mentally because it's a time for purposeful thinking. Busy mothers need times of quiet contemplation.

The Benefits of Quiet Time

There are many benefits to having time alone with God. It was not until I had my children that my quiet time took a dive—just when I needed it the most! I've spoken with new converts who are moms and who profess they do not even know what quiet time is. It's even harder to have quiet

> **Quiet time is not about performing some systematic religious duty, but about cultivating a relationship with our Creator. It is a most personal matter.**

time if you never engaged in the discipline before your children were born, because it is a discipline and, like all disciplines, must be cultivated.

Quiet time is not about performing some systematic religious duty but about cultivating a relationship with our Creator. It is a most personal matter. I would never tell a wife how to love her husband or minister personally to her family, so in this chapter I will not attempt to tell you what to do in your quiet time. I simply want to encourage you to press into the discipline. My greatest spiritual growth has been the result of my time alone with God.

Even my family can tell when I haven't had my quiet time, because they usually get the overflow of patience, kindness, and long-suffering that comes from it. Once I have had time to fill up, then I can respond out of my spiritual overflow. Most times, when we are short-tempered or short on patience, we are usually short on quiet time. Great men and women of the faith, and even Jesus himself, engaged in the discipline of solitude. Jesus regularly got away from the crowd.

The real results of quiet time occur over the long haul. Sometimes we can go day to day not realizing how bereft we are without it. I know when I was a young mom, if I missed my quiet time in the morning, I would just consider it gone. I legalistically thought quiet time was only for the morning, and if I didn't get a chance to have it, I was empty for the day. However, the Lord began to show me other creative ways to get quiet time.

Naptime makes an excellent quiet time. Family quiet hour also works for us. During quiet hour, everyone has to be quiet for a specified time. They can read books. Little

Tips for a Profitable Quiet Time

- Place items you will be using during your morning quiet time together at night.
- Read a segment of what you will be reading during your quiet time before you go to bed.
- Use a basket for holding your quiet time items if you do not have a room or space you can use for quiet time.
- Talk to others about your quiet time.
- Journal before, during, and after your quiet time, if desired.
- Specify a goal in your quiet time.

ones can play silently with special quiet-time toys that they only get to play with during family quiet time. I have even had my quiet time while I watched the kids on the swing set in the backyard.

I'm a staunch advocate of early-morning quiet time, but if you miss it or simply are not a morning person, I'd rather you try some creative alternatives than forfeit quiet time altogether. Some moms actually get babysitters or trade child care with one another so they can have quiet time. Homeschooling moms may also fast during lunch and pray during meal times. This is especially effective if you do not let your children have any snacks and as an added bonus provide them with their favorite lunch, because kids will want to spend more time at the table, which translates into more quiet time for you.

A regular ten or fifteen minutes a day is better than no time at all. Adaptability is key, although early morning may be difficult, especially if you haven't had a full night of sleep. God knows your heart. So be encouraged to have quiet time, even if it's as simple as every morning sitting up in bed acknowledging God. Ask him to be with you. Of course, even if you don't ask him, he is there.

Meet You There, Lord

There are other ways to ensure you are consistent with your quiet time. None of these suggestions are meant to induce guilt or to be used legalistically. These are simply things that have worked for me.

Most moms do not plan enough for their devotionals. This is not an indictment against moms; we spend so much time planning for everything else, we just assume quiet time will happen.

Set spiritual goals for your quiet time. Share your personal revelations with your husband, your children, and other moms. Get another mom as an accountability partner. Basically, I'm saying make it a priority.

Give your children the heritage of seeing you pray for them. Let them see you come to God. You'll be amazed at how this will motivate your children to establish their own time alone with God. Let them see you enthusiastically run to God.

Come to him as your counselor. Bring your family and marriage concerns to him. Come to him as your friend. Bring your emotional, mental, and spiritual needs. Come to him as your provider. Come to him as your Lord. Bring him all your concerns.

Planning begins long before your scheduled quiet time. Choose a room or uninterrupted space. Designate a whole room if you can. At one point, we actually had a quiet room in our home where everyone could have quiet time. We merely had to be aware of one another's schedules. If you don't have a room, then designate a specific place where you will have quiet time every day.

Early morning is ideal for quiet time. Family members are still asleep; thus, you're unlikely to be interrupted. It also sets the tone for your day. Mothers with young children, who may not be sleeping completely through the

More Tips for a Profitable Quiet Time

- Early morning is a prime time for quiet time.
- If you miss your quiet time in the morning, then just do it later.
- Personalize your quiet time.
- If you continually miss quiet time, ask yourself why you want to do it and why you do not want to do it.
- Get an image of what you see yourself receiving from your quiet time.
- Allow no interruptions at all. This especially applies to children. Train them to leave you alone during your quiet time.
- Prepare the room you will be having quiet time in so that you are not distracted.
- Keep your notes from your quiet time organized.

night, may alter this a bit. These moms may find it better to have quiet time in the evenings or during naptime. Even if you do not have a full quiet-time regimen in the mornings, you should still take time to acknowledge God before you begin your day.

Quiet time is hard work, and you'll need the right tools. I have a large-print Bible, various Bible translations, Bible dictionary, Bible concordance (*Strong's* and *Young's* are my standards for Bible study), journal, devotional book, notepad, planner, and facial tissues (for those misty moments). I put these items in a small storage container. You can get these containers at almost any convenience store like Wal-Mart for a few dollars. Most people use them to store small clothing or items. I transport the container wherever I go. I use my container as if it were a traveling altar, because my home is so small and I don't have space for one designated spot to engage in quiet time. I used to have a big basket.

93

It definitely was more feminine but eventually could not hold all my quiet-time materials.

The container has helped to bring a sense of stability to my quiet time. At times I even kneel to pray and use the container as a personal altar. You may also use a large wicker basket or whatever appeals to you. My container with its tight lid keeps little prying hands out. The important thing is you have all your quiet-time materials in one spot. You are more effective if you don't have to run around the house looking for everything.

The other thing you can do is prime yourself for your quiet time. Get excited about it. Do not view it as a chore. Think about this: the Creator of the universe is ready to personally meet with you.

Expect God to be right there in your kitchen. Place an empty chair at your table as a reminder. Put your quiet-time materials out the night before. Open your Bible or devotional book to the chapter you will read the next morning. Glance at it. Pray about your quiet time as you drift off to sleep.

There are other things you may do to encourage a consistent quiet time, and they're so simple you'll wonder why you missed them. Make quiet time as pleasant as possible. Sit down in the morning with a steeping cup of herbal tea and some crackers, or do a bit of exercise first. My husband jogs early in the morning and talks with God. Go on a prayer walk.

Journal. Get a nice journal and write letters to God. Ask him to write back to you, and expect God to give you answers to your prayers. Most importantly, express your frustrations to God and ask him to give you creative strategies to have quiet time. Tell him how much you miss being with him. I know he misses you. He calls out to us, but sometimes we drown out his voice in our busyness.

What Were You Saying, Lord?

Let's be real, ladies. Sometimes we have used our children and housework to drown out his voice. We don't necessarily do it on purpose, but we get more affirmation from outward works than from the inward discipline of silence in quiet time. Silence forces us to press in beyond our understanding to admit our shortcomings. We do not always see the results of spending private time with God immediately, but we can see our neatly vacuumed carpet. That gives us a sense of accomplishment. Our performance mode keeps us away from God as we realize there is nothing we can give him but ourselves.

Sometimes we have used our children and housework to drown out his voice because we get more affirmation from outward works than from the inward discipline of silence.

The things we can do distract us from God. I'm sure you have prayed and had other things enter your mind indiscriminately. How do you deal with it? Most of us feel guilty and spend our prayer time either repenting or attempting to cast out the thought. But our minds were given to us to bless us, and rather than working against your mind, you can work with it. Here's what you do: the next time you're in quiet time and a thought crosses your mind, write it down, and then quickly return to praying. You will find that when you write it down, your mind says, "Okay, she remembers that," and will be quiet. I have also noticed that if I write a reasonable to-do list with scheduled events the night prior to my quiet time, those thoughts do not occur often.

In chapter 2, we talked about the importance of setting the atmosphere of your home. Atmosphere can help or hinder your time alone with God. Do not have quiet time in a room that is typically noisy or messy. Besides distracting you with clutter and disorder, the room will breed disordered thoughts. Let's face it, we all think better in clean and orderly environments, and we pray better in clean and orderly environments. You can with practice condition yourself to tune out distractions, but that just makes quiet time more laborious.

You will find that distractions diminish as you continue quiet time regularly. So press in. Enjoy nature or the outdoors. Being in the middle of God's creation helps to focus our minds on the Lord. Try sitting on the porch or looking out a window. Being tired can also be a distraction, which means you need to get enough rest.

Physical ailments and stress can encumber our time alone with God too. A racing mind may be calmed by soft, meditative music. Upbeat praise and worship music can turn a sullen temperament around. The lad David played his harp so melodiously that he lifted the tormented Saul's mood. We likewise can use music in our quiet time to help us focus on God.

We may be distracted by our sin. We feel unworthy to come into God's presence. We fear he will reprimand us. Or because of low self-esteem, we think he really does not want to spend time with us. Others of us have such an awesome fear of God that we question why he would commune with us. Or we feel we will get alone with God and have nothing to say. Take all these concerns to God. It may be a great way to honestly begin your quiet time.

The children of Israel walked to Mount Horeb, but when they saw the smoke engulfing the mountain, they feared God speaking to them. The strange thing was that God was with them all the time. He was leading them by a pillar of cloud during the day and a pillar of fire by night. He was there all along. He wanted greater intimacy, but the children of Israel refused to step into his presence. They sent Moses to speak to God for them. It is said that the children of Israel knew God's acts, but Moses knew his ways.

I'm Here Now, So What Do I Do?

As I always tell my children, you will never learn anything of substance in a crowd. Psychologists have long documented that a crowd mentality will cause otherwise

You will never learn anything of substance in a crowd.

sane people to do the unmentionable—even to the point of going against their own beliefs. The very crowd that cried hosanna to the King of Kings would one week later cry, "Crucify him!"

Quiet time is imperative for Christians because it helps us keep from being overrun by others' thoughts and opinions. This is especially true for those of us who attend a lot of church services or who listen to Christian radio all day. Subtly, others begin to form our thoughts for us, and we may not be aware of the influence of relentless Christian programming, which causes us to acquiesce to the thoughts and opinions of others in more esteemed positions than us. If we do not read our Bible for ourselves, we will always see it in the light of another's interpretation. We will therefore never have our own perspective.

Scripture should be read in context. It's a great discipline to practice reading whole books at a time, perhaps using your study time to research the historic context of the passages. Psalms may be read for comfort. The book of Proverbs may be read for wisdom. You may also pray Scripture back to God—just as my children come to me and remind me of what I have said. It warms my heart that they listen to me and trust that what I say is true. I'm sure God likes us to have confidence in him too.

Sincerely seek the heart of God for Scripture on which to meditate. Sometimes we think we know the problem and search for a Scripture to be in agreement with what we want. Once I was praying for my daughter's healing and found a litany of healing Scriptures, but one day God

Even More Tips for a Profitable Quiet Time

- Make certain the atmosphere is set before your quiet time begins. Play soft music.
- Avoid having quiet time in an area of the house associated with conflict and noise, even when your scheduled quiet time does not occur at that time. The overall atmosphere affects you.
- Have specific goals for what you want out of your quiet time.
- Write your prayers on five- by eight-inch index cards so you can hold them and not be distracted during prayer.
- Pray over photographs of loved ones. This will help you focus in prayer.
- Cut newspaper clippings if you are praying about national events.
- Write down the names of your local elected officials so you can pray for them during your quiet time.

impressed upon my heart that the issue was not his healing her. The greater issue was that he wanted me to trust him. Therefore, I found Scriptures to meditate on in the area of trust. The obvious was not so obvious to me, and I am convinced I would not have made the connection without time alone with God. We are utterly transformed when we get alone with God. He tells us personal things as he pulls back the covers from our hearts and the blinders from our eyes.

Meditation must be engaged in during quiet time. It's different from Bible reading in that without meditation the truth we know will not affect us. As a man or woman thinks, so is he or she. Much of our time alone with God is simply a matter of transforming our thoughts so our behavior can be changed.

Memorization is also part of the process. Our quiet time solidifies the Scripture so the Holy Spirit can bring it back to our remembrance when we need it the most. You may even set Scripture to music to help memorize it. I have done this with my children, especially when memorizing large blocks of Scripture.

Quiet time is a time of prayer. Praying for others helps us to be God focused. Writing down your prayers helps you focus on them. The book *Prayers That Avail Much for Mothers*, by Germaine Copeland, has helped jump-start my prayers. Copeland takes the Scriptures and weaves them together. It truly is anointed prayer, because it is the promises of the Bible put in prayer form.

Praying is not asking God for things all the time but waiting to hear what he will say to you. Be careful not to plan your quiet time so rigorously that God cannot change the program. Be sensitive to persistent thoughts that keep coming back to you, especially after you have written them down. Is God telling you to do something? Ask him!

Brother Lawrence, in his classic book *The Practice of the Presence of God*, points out that our minds will not wander in our quiet time if we do not allow our minds to wander at other times. Practice purposeful thinking. Watch what you are thinking about all the time, as it affects your quiet time. It is therefore a good practice to think on that which is pure, lovely, and of good report, as that renders our hearts available to receive the Word of God.

It may be obvious, but quiet time means being quiet. I say this because silence forces us to listen. Quiet time is where we meet personally, face-to-face with God. True, we can rarely block out all the noise, but as we concentrate and daily press in to know him, it gets easier as it becomes habit. And like Elijah, we learn God is not in the whirlwind but in the still, small voice.

I encourage moms to journal so that we can document our time with God. This is not to be done out of drudgery but only if you really enjoy writing about your time with

God. Get a nice journal. Journaling is effective because it forces you to sit down and really be quiet. Granted, quiet time means many things to many people, but we can all agree it does require us being quiet. This includes being quiet in our thoughts and assured that God is not angry with us. In fact, he is very excited about spending time alone with us. Yes, he enjoys being with us in our everyday activities, but he also enjoys time spent solely with us.

What Are You Thinking, God?

Perhaps we really should be praying that we have ears to hear and hearts to understand what the Lord is saying to us. Perhaps even the enemy knows the power of quiet time and keeps us moms away from it. Perhaps the enemy knows the power of our prayers for ourselves and our children. Perhaps we need to discipline ourselves to accomplish this awesome task. We need a vision for success in our quiet time. We need a revelation of God. We need God's perspective.

So how do we do it? First, never assume God is angry with you. He stands with outstretched arms to welcome you into his presence. He yearns to hug you. Aren't you glad his faithfulness is divine? He does not do things by man's standards.

When I was composing this book, my home was a mess. I was lamenting my predicament one afternoon, and being highly unproductive, when a friend called. As I was speaking to her about my home being messy and the kids deciding whether or not they should declare a liberation coup and telephone Grandma to get a real meal, I blurted out, "People who came in my house at this moment would surely tell me to give it all up because I am a failure."

100

But the important question, she reasoned, was, "Did God tell you to do this project at this time? Do you think he is mad at you?"

Of course not! I knew God was not mad at me, but I had let my unreasonable expectations of myself affect my perception of God. I repented and was able to minister to my family in quite creative ways. Actually, the coup was suppressed by a delivery of pizza with extra cheese. I was able to put my focus back on God. It's our own screwed-up perceptions of God that often affect how we view him and what we do in quiet time.

Years ago I heard a powerful message, "Could You Not Tarry for One Hour?" taken from Matthew 26:40, in which Jesus's disciples fell asleep on him. He asked them, "Could you not watch with Me one hour?" (NKJV). After hearing that message, I became convinced I should pray for at least an hour a day, and it had to be before daybreak, because I read in Scripture how Jesus got up early and went off to pray.

Every day at the stroke of five I would drag myself out of my bed to do my perceived Christian duty. It was obvious: I was not enjoying my quiet time. I would crawl into my prayer room and start reciting the prayer I thought the Lord wanted to hear. One day the Lord impressed on me that he was not enjoying it either. He took no joy out of me being there because I had to be there. He wanted me to run to his arms like a little child who longs to be with him. I was forced to make some adjustments.

The bottom line is that we serve God with willing and grateful hearts. I'm sure someone will say, "But Cheryl, if you encourage moms to have a quiet time every day, aren't you getting them to concentrate on works rather than relationship?" This is always possible. Any routine can become dry and lifeless after a while, but it's easier to ask God to resurrect a dead routine than to discipline ourselves to establish the habit.

Finally, Jesus really understands us moms. He was followed everywhere he went and had to steal away from the crowds. He was even interrupted during his quiet time. In Mark 1:35–39, Jesus rose early and went to a solitary place to pray. Simon and Jesus's disciples searched for him. There is no record in Scripture that he got angry with them or rebuked them. Rather, he went with them to minister. As moms, there will surely be times when our time with God will be interrupted, but we must still press on to serve our husbands and children with good attitudes.

Having a quiet time does not make you a better Christian. Dying to yourself is what makes you Christlike. The ritual of quiet time can be just another religious tradition you do to get a proverbial pin on your Christian suit. The real issue is transformation. Your quiet time must affect all your time. It is not a Christian duty, it is a privilege. We have access to the King of Kings. May it transform us.

Keys to Successful Quiet Time

Quiet time is a personal discipline, but it is also a personal relationship. Therein is the sticky point. Some, especially extroverts who are used to spending time in a crowd, fear they will be alone with God and not know what to say. Others, under the cloak of guilt, shame, or condemnation, enter his presence with dread. Still others, due to relational issues with other people, see God, both consciously and unconsciously, in the dysfunction of their relationships. So while we know we should come to the Creator, we struggle with what to do once we are in his presence—and some of us wonder if he will even show up. These issues take time and must be dealt with honestly and passionately. We cannot deny our thoughts and fears.

All relationships are built on trust, and we must first confess our faults to the Lord and ask him to give us a knowledge of and a zeal for him. We must come to our time alone with him with expectancy. We also must resolve that we will indeed come. Self-discipline comes in stages. It all starts with a decision.

A decision seems simple enough, but it is more than resolve. It involves your acknowledging the things you will give up to have a consistent quiet time. Giving our time to God every day involves giving up something, and we have to be honest with ourselves. Our decision must not be made in zeal but with prayerful reflection, or else we won't stick with it.

After we make a decision, we prepare for our quiet time. You may purchase a basket or put all your quiet-time materials together. Pray and begin. Reward yourself for the little steps you make along the way. Speak positively to yourself. Say things like, "Cheryl, you're doing a good job getting up early." If you sleep in one day, do not berate yourself; just continue to encourage yourself to keep trying. Positive remarks to ourselves are also a way to renew our minds and help us to expectantly enter God's presence. Adequate preparation will assist you in keeping up your quiet time.

The performance stage is next. There are primarily four ways the enemy will keep you from your quiet time. He will tell you, "If you missed it, just forget it." This will occur when you are up all night with the kids or the stomach virus runs through the house. Stay focused. If you miss your quiet time in the morning, meditate throughout the day and have it midday or in the evening.

Performance anxiety, believing that everything must be perfect, will also keep you from your time alone with the Lord. Do not fall for this trap. Even if everyone isn't asleep or the house isn't perfectly quiet, still get alone with the Lord. Do not wait for your favorite Bible to come parcel

Possible Contents for Your Quiet-Time Basket

- Pens/pencils
- Study or devotional Bibles
- Mothers' devotional
- Journal or notebooks
- Bible concordances and Bible dictionary
- Prayer cards or prayer list
- Photographs of loved ones you are praying for
- Mothers' prayer books
- Tissues (for those misty moments)
- Quiet worship music with portable CD player
- Husband's prayer requests

post or to buy a new basket; come as you are to the Lord. Now is the time to seek him.

It is hard work to come to the Lord, silence our thoughts, and be with him. Do not let the labor of quiet time overshadow the benefits. Even those steeped in the discipline will confide that it is hard work, especially in the beginning, as you are establishing the habit.

Also, do not fall for the enemy's lies that you are too busy, lazy, or stupid to change. Everyone can change. You are a new creation in Christ Jesus. These lies and others are used because quiet time is one of your best allies to be conformed to the image of Christ. Get Scripture and battle these lies. Talk to yourself. David encouraged himself in the Lord. He spoke the truth and listened to himself and was able to win the battle. Get that? David actually listened to himself (1 Sam. 30:6).

To reinforce your efforts, continue to speak positively to yourself, and reward yourself for consistent quiet time. Eventually, quiet time will become a reward in itself. Make a reward list for yourself. Be very specific about what you will give yourself. Get a vision: see yourself in quiet time being successful. Talk to yourself and encourage yourself along the way. Keep saying you can do it. Use Scripture and ask God for his help. You cannot do it alone. Finally, learn to relax and enjoy the process. Do not rush around before quiet time; enter it peacefully, relaxed, with a calmness that helps set the atmosphere. Ask the Lord for his peace.

Is It Time for You to Be Quiet?

Americans are the biggest consumers in the world. Our national and consumer debt bears this truth out. Our present electronic age has also fostered a hurried lifestyle. We have beepers, cell phones, pagers, and Internet organizers—just so someone can reach out and touch us. We have become a society abuzz with activity, obsessed with doing things. This mind-set has become part of our culture, so we shouldn't be surprised that it has infiltrated the church.

Rushing is really the result of industrialized nations and their zeal to do more, have more, and be more. Remember the story from chapter 4 about the American missionaries on assignment in Africa? The missionaries tiredly arose early, expecting their African guides to be up. Instead, they found them fast asleep. When the missionaries questioned how the guides could sleep so soundly after such a powerful meeting the night before, the guides replied, "We need time for our bodies to catch up with our souls." How profound! The guides understood they could not demand more of themselves until they slowed down, rested, and took time to be still.

Stillness is not truly appreciated in our society. Even though the Scripture "Be still, and know that I am God" (Psalm 46:10) may be quoted in most churches, the implication is that we stand still and have our rallies, missionary

"Be still, and know that I am God."
Psalm 46:10

dinners, praise and worship clinics, guest speakers, and Fun Friday youth nights. In short, we say we're waiting on God when in reality we're working our plan and waiting for God to bless it. Understand, I have no qualms with any church program, but too often it is born of the flesh and not of the Spirit. Simply put, programs are human-devised plans to Band-Aid a perceived wound in the church instead of letting God truly heal the lesion. Programs are not inherently wrong, but too often rather than putting in the time to pray through to a solution, we just come to our conclusions and move full speed ahead. For instance, God may place it on our heart to minister to homeless people. Immediately, instead of seeking God and getting wise counsel, zeal causes us to rally people in the church to start a soup kitchen. However, if we had prayed a bit longer, we might have realized that the homeless need more than a meal: they need a plan to get them out of their despair. It may be that a homeless ministry that addresses work skills, negative mind-sets, and substance abuse might be more of what was on God's heart.

Too often we are like King Saul, who looked at the coming battle and devised his own plans instead of heeding the words of Samuel the prophet (1 Samuel 15). Somehow, we have the same mistaken notion that we must be doing something for God to act on our behalf. Yet remember the way Elisha prayed for his servant Gehazi, "Open his eyes." Once his eyes were opened, the servant saw the military host of the Lord poised for battle on his master's behalf (2 Kings 6:17). A lot of us need to pray to have our eyes opened to see what God is doing in the spirit realm.

Our society's preoccupation with activity has followed us into our prayer closets. So many Christians spend their quiet time with the Lord in anything but quiet. They wail, quote, and cry—when God is saying, "Listen." You cannot listen when you are talking, crying, or singing to the Lord. Catch this great spiritual principle: to hear God speak, you have to be quiet! Sounds simple, but to practice the discipline of silence is truly a virtue.

The kind of silence I'm talking about does not involve your asking God a question, then hovering on your knees as you wait for his response so you can get up and go. I remember in Sunday school being taught that God answers in three ways—yes, no, and wait awhile. Well, I have a surprise for you: God has more than those three responses in his repertoire. He is our personal Lord and Savior and interacts with us personally, not according to a prescribed plan of man. We need to approach God and just be silent.

Too often our personal time with God is spent asking him for things. For the next seven days, go to prayer without an agenda and watch what happens.

Too often our personal time with God is spent asking him to bless us instead of communing with him. I offer a challenge. For the next seven days, go to prayer without an agenda. Just ask God what he wants to talk to you about. Allot some time to hear him. You may be quite surprised at what God wants to talk about.

God is not interested in your getting a new car. He is not concerned that Sister Bobbie Lou didn't speak to you. He isn't even concerned that the choir members have been coming late to rehearsal recently. He *is* concerned about your attitude toward money. Has the prosperity message been out of balance in your life? He may ask you why you haven't prayed for Sister Bobbie Lou's brother who has AIDS. He may tell you to lay hands on the sick at choir rehearsal next week. He may talk to you about your secret sin—you know, the one you hide behind your religious piety.

Being silent and waiting for God to speak is hard. Sometimes our environment is quiet but our minds are racing. We think about the unpaid bill or the piece of lint on the carpet we've been meaning to vacuum.

Other times our own thoughts and desires are louder than God. My three-year-old daughter will often come and ask me if she can have a cookie while the cookie is in her hand. Her eyes are fixated on the cookie, and she is really just asking me so she can say she was being obedient. She's rather cute as she smells the cookie and brings it close to her mouth as she anticipates my positive response. When I tell her no, which I do often, since I enjoy seeing her response, she pauses. The cookie remains close to her mouth as she persuades me to let her have the cookie. It is like she just cannot hear my no.

We are like that with God sometimes. We ask the Lord questions out of Christian duty and religious tradition, but we really do not want to hear his true response. It takes time to quiet our own desires so we can hear God. That is why I call silence a discipline. We have to work at it daily, particularly in our culture, which regularly invades our quiet time. We need to practice being quiet before the Lord each day. Start out in little increments. Pray and ask the Lord to help you develop the discipline of silence.

God is calling Christians to drop their religious traditions and to be silent before him. Perhaps you have had some issues before the Lord, and he is telling you to put down the cookie so he can discuss the real issue with you—your attitude, your prejudices, or your critical tongue. Perhaps God is saying, "I have called you as a prophet to this nation." Perhaps God is saying, "I have called you to speak loud and spare not." Perhaps God is saying, "It is time to leave your old dead traditions and receive a fresh anointing of my Spirit." Perhaps God is beckoning you to come up to the mountain of his presence. Be quiet and listen. Do you hear him? He is calling you!

Prayer

Lord, I hear you!

6

Catching Up with God

In His Presence, the Exhilaration of the Chase

As moms, we often feel our jobs are less than divine. After all, our lives are spent dealing with dirty dishes, grimy laundry, messy spills, and smelly bathrooms. What can be divine about that? Intellectually, we know that God is omnipresent, and therefore, we accept that he must be there with us. But this is mere mental assent, as we often struggle to get our heads above water until the next time we can have time alone with the Lord. We want God, but often he just seems so distant in our everyday lives.

We begin to lean on our time alone with God. We are assured we will meet with him there. However, some of us struggle, even in our quiet time, to feel the presence of God. We have quiet time out of a sense of Christian duty or service, but we get no joy out of it, except for the occasional religious rush we get when we check it off our to-do list.

The problem did not begin in our prayer closets. It began in our daily lives, in the choices we made, the thoughts we allowed to run rampant in our minds, and the attitudes we allowed to become strongholds in our decision-making process. It is our daily lives that must be dealt with first.

One of my favorite books is *The Practice of the Presence of God*. This classic, written by Brother Lawrence, is ripe with godly insight and blessing. He was a monk in the 1600s who was known to experience God's presence daily. He said, and I paraphrase for the sake of clarity, that after his personal time with God, he applied his mind carefully to the rest of the day and, even in the midst of his business, to the presence of God, when he considered God was "always with me, often in me."

Now before you dismiss the notion, let's look at the biblical precedence for such a thought. The children of Israel experienced God's presence in the pillar of cloud by day and the pillar of fire by night. Acts 17:28 declares, "In him we live and move and have our being." Christ is not in a cloud. In this dispensation, the Lord has taken residence in our hearts, and we can live in his presence daily.

God's Presence in Our Daily Lives

"Okay, Cheryl, how can I do this?" you ask. Invite God into the process. The neat thing about God is that he is not like us. We tell our children to clean their rooms, and by golly, they'd better clean their rooms by the time we come in and check. God tells us to clean up our act, then offers to come in and help us. Makes you rethink some of your parenting decisions, huh? Often we hear a sermon or message or read a good book and struggle to implement suggestions we know will change our lives. God gives us information that helps us make the right choice, then equips us to make that choice.

Set your minds on things above, not on earthly things.

Colossians 3:2

Scripture is ripe with examples of this. Deuteronomy 28, the infamous chapter—or famous, depending on whether you look at the glass as half filled or half empty—talks about the blessing God will give his people and the curses, or negative consequences, of their own sin if they make the wrong choice. He gives Israel the choice, then he says, "Choose life, so that you and your children may live" (Deut. 30:19). He instructs us like a good parent and almost forces us to make the right choice.

I remember when Derek used to drive fast—well before children, and in his youth. When we were first married, he drove a Honda Accord. I think this was before the Accord craze was on. Anyway, one day we were going to his cousin's home for a barbecue. There was a stretch of land where it was pretty safe to drive fast, and needless to say, Derek would accelerate a bit on those streets. On this particular day, as he started down this street, he saw his mom's car in the middle of the road. Naturally, he slowed down. "Mom, what are you doing here?" he pried.

"I saw this big hole in the road, and I knew if you came down too fast, you'd damage your car," she said, then added almost apologetically, "Of course, I know you don't drive fast."

She was there to stop him from hurting himself by his own youthful zeal. God is like that with us. He protects us from ourselves at times. God is constantly giving opportunities like that to us. However, we often look for God to show up in the spectacular or just in our quiet time. God knew how much that car meant to Derek and put the desire in his mother's heart to save him from the pain of regret. We too have done the same for our children on various levels.

Derek's response to his mother also would make the difference as to whether or not her presence there was a blessing. He could have chosen to get angry and deny that he had a

Our reward for serving God is that we receive more of him.

tendency to speed, but he did not. Keep this in mind. Our response to God will always determine our blessing.

He Is Waiting to Be Found

In 2 Chronicles 15, we learn a powerful principle about God. When we seek him, he is there for us. Asa, after a successful battle, decides to reform Israel. Actually, he wants to turn Israel back to God. Azariah comes to Asa and, in verse 2, says, "The LORD is with you when you are with him. If you seek him, he will be found by you, but if you forsake him, he will forsake you." In verse 4, we see Israel makes the right choice to seek God, "and he was found by them." God rewards the nation of Israel because they sought him. We must seek God with our whole heart, and he will reward us. Remember, though, our reward is that we receive more of him.

We moms need to seek the Lord daily. We have no choice. I know this seems hard. It is! Yet the rewards are so great. Often we are stressed and encumbered with so much that we do not realize in handling it ourselves we have made the decision to go it alone. We have to make a quality decision to seek after God. We must practice purposeful thinking where every thought is directed to God.

As you read 2 Chronicles 15, you will see Israel took action by removing the "detestable idols from the whole land" (v. 8). Once they made a decision to seek the Lord, they never turned back. In verse 12, we see once again (refer-

We moms need to seek the Lord daily. ring back to v. 4) how the people "entered into a covenant to seek the LORD, the God of their fathers, with all their heart and soul." These folks were serious, and if you read the whole chapter, you will see they were tremendously blessed!

Notice in 2 Chronicles 15:2, the first step to experiencing God's presence and favor in our daily lives is to know the Lord is with us while we are with him. Yes, we know God is omnipresent, but I am referring to his being present in our day-to-day activities as much as he is present in our prayer closet or a corporate church service.

Seeking God's presence is not always a conscious choice we make, nor am I implying that moms are more inherently evil than others. Moms are just like everyone else. Sometimes we do the right thing, and sometimes we do the wrong thing. We long for the presence of God, but we hold on to old habits, thought patterns, and sin when God is calling to us to give them up. Yes, we have to admit we have not made a quality decision to have him be part of our days. I know I have been guilty of this and must constantly remind myself not to lean on past victories or my own intellect.

Even the powerful times in our quiet time can become an idol to us, if what was obtained there does not become part of our nature. By nature, and Western culture, we are independent beings who resist authority and restraint. Therefore, daily we have to earnestly come to God and say, "Today, I will follow you. Help make me willing." It is an attitude of the heart that will cultivate blessings.

I know some of you are saying, "But it all sounds too simple. Would God really show up on the scene because I ask him to come?" It is not just the words but the earnestness of your heart. God would be unjust if he doesn't do as he has promised.

Some of us do not recognize how bereft we are until we hit bottom. God does not want us to hit bottom, but we have to want to seek him. He merely waits for us to get to the end of ourselves and cry out to him. When you recognize you can be nothing without him, that only he has the power to change you, and that all your righteousness is as filthy rags, then, when you cry out to him in helpless abandon and faith, he will answer you. Isaiah says, "This is the one I esteem: he who is humble and contrite in spirit, and trembles at my word" (66:2). He has promised to do so! Of course, I hope you know I am not implying you get on the floor and cry your lungs out; I am talking about a posture of repentance.

Often we have been led to believe that once we go to the altar and make a confession of salvation, our repenting days are over. Nothing could be further from the truth.

I'm Sorry, Lord

Repentance means a changing of your mind and heart. Often we have been led to believe that once we go to the altar and make a confession of salvation, our repenting days are over. Nothing could be further from the truth. Our decision to accept Christ is the first big decision; but as we walk with God and are transformed into his image, we will find that truly repentance is a lifestyle. Even if we accepted the Lord as children, we have wrong mind-sets, bad attitudes, and sin that must be dealt with on a regular basis.

When Derek and I do family workshops, we often ask a foundational question: "What makes you a Christian?" Generally, the responses are "Christlike," "know God," "a King's kid," and so on; but when I press people for what it means, few can really tell us. This isn't necessarily a bad thing if we are so wrapped up in relationship with God that we cannot adequately describe our commitment to him. For instance, I love Derek, but if you ask me why I love him, I could not identify any one reason. I just do! My love for him is unconditional. If I loved him for any specific thing and that thing ever changed, that would put our love in jeopardy. Instead, I love him without measure. Do you see why God compared our marriage relationships to our relationship to him?

Loving someone is not a static thing. There is no formula to it. When we love someone, we become more like the one we are in love with. Friends often relay that talking to Derek or me is like speaking with the other. Over the years, I have adopted more of Derek's attributes, and he has taken on mine. There have been areas in both of our lives that we have had to die to so that our marriage could grow into oneness. It is similar in our relationship with the Lord. We must become less like ourselves in order to be more like God.

Clearly, being a Christian means daily dying to self so that the life of Christ can consume me. Simply put, it is being transformed into God's image. We are to be transformed in our thoughts, our motives, and the intents of our hearts. Even though we give sacrificially, and as moms we are born givers, we can sometimes unfortunately find our identity and accolades in the ministry of motherhood. This too will cause us to miss God. We must be squarely established in the love of God in order to serve with a pure heart. It all begins with a decision.

The Lord is with you while you are with him. Once we make the decision to be with the Lord, the Holy Spirit, who energizes us to get in step with God, helps us move in the direction of that righteous decision. So we say, "God, I want to know you. I want to experience you in my everyday life."

Take the time now to repent. Tell the Lord you want more of him and less of you. You have to die to yourself to grow in the love of God. You have to want to look more like him than yourself. That's a hard decision to make, but one that offers great reward. Make a decision to seek him daily and to live a life of repentance.

Repentance is a touchy subject for us, because we like to be right, and the Lord is constantly telling us our thoughts are not like his thoughts. Most of the time we are unaware of our true motives. Once I was bragging on my daughter's published article and the Lord showed me that my admiration of my daughter's writing had degenerated into pride. The truth was, others speaking well of my daughter's work was validating me, especially since I had not accomplished such a feat. Interestingly, I often advise parents not to do this, but I had fallen into the sin of beholding a minor beam in others' eyes and not seeing the obvious log in my own eye.

We have to be careful in projecting our own issues on our children. We toilet train them early because the books all say they should be toilet trained by three. Never mind that your child is not emotionally ready. We want them to take piano lessons because *we* wanted to be a virtuoso. Even our sacrificial acts of service can have wrong motives. The Lord must show us ourselves so that we may repent and serve our families in the power and presence of the Lord. When God's love flows through us, it is pure and peaceable.

This may seem rather obvious, but isn't it true that we see others' flaws more easily than our own? I am not advocating that you get so introspective that you become depressed and discouraged. There is joy in serving God, and when he promises you or tells you to do something, get ready for a miracle. Be happy, because something great is about to happen!

Every time Jesus told people to do something, no matter how insignificant, when his hand was on it, it was magnified. He took a little boy's lunch and fed a multitude. He

Ways to Combine the Divine with the Familiar

- Pray for your family while ironing their clothes, washing dishes, folding laundry, and so on.
- Make a gratitude journal. Challenge yourself nightly to find things God has uniquely done to bless you that day.
- Pray back posted Scripture to the Lord while you're doing household tasks like vacuuming and cleaning.
- Write Scripture on index cards and take it with you during your commute or lunchtime.
- Put a Scripture verse on your computer screen saver.
- Sing praises and hymns as you go through your day. If you work in an environment where it's okay to disengage, then invest in headphones.

could have summoned enough fish out of the sea to feed the congregation, but he chose to use a little boy. Moms, he is not asking us for much. He just wants us to give the little we have to him.

God, I Know You Are Here

That was almost too easy, you say. Well, stay with me. The next step is probably the hardest for mothers: we have to seek him daily in our everyday routine. You have to consciously stop several times in your day and become aware of God. You know he's there, so you just have to discipline yourself to see him. "Whoa, Cheryl! How do I do that?" Simple. You ask for his help and begin to look for things in your environment that will turn your thoughts to him.

As you read in chapter 4, all the rooms in your home should have Scripture throughout. If you have not done this, please take the time to post Scripture everywhere you can in your home. Make it a priority. These Scriptures will remind you to seek God. Enlist the help of your children. Ask them to look to see the hand of God in their lives too.

When you do see his hand, thank him. Gratitude confirms relationship. Thankfulness is also a good way to deal with ungratefulness in our sin nature. Thankfulness is a way to welcome the presence of God in the little details of your day. Psalm 95:2 encourages us to enter his presence with thanksgiving. We are further exhorted to "enter into his gates with thanksgiving, and into his courts with praise: be thankful unto him, and bless his name" (Ps. 100:4 KJV).

Being thankful on a daily basis ushers in God's presence. Take time to write down the blessings you see or to collectively share them with your family. Perhaps you can think of special things God has done for you that day and have your kids make pictures. Even teenagers would benefit from this exercise, as they are often so regimented to church service that they do not necessarily see God as being real or relevant to their lives.

A lifestyle of praise and worship is what we really need to see God even more clearly. We sing praise and worship songs in church, or we may even listen to worshipful music, but how many of us live lives of praise and worship? Scripture affirms that God inhabits the praises of his people (Ps. 22:3). He inhabits our praises in the activities of our daily lives. Praise invites God into any situation. Loosely defined, *praise* in Hebrew means "a narrative to God," a kind of talking back to him of his goodness. Praising him helps us to see him more clearly.

On the other hand, *worship*, which is equally important and usually relegated to quiet meditative songs in our services, means expressing reverence or devotion. I'm sure all you Hebrew and Greek scholars out there are shuddering a bit at my simplistic definition, but stay with me. We praise God when we sincerely and fervently talk back to him and tell others of his goodness or faithful deeds. Some do it in music, but our lives are an orchestra to God.

God blesses us every day; therefore, we should be praising him every day. Once when I was teaching Sunday school
(grades five and six), I assigned the kids the task of looking
for things to daily thank God for. The first week they came
in with rather superficial stuff, often repeating one another.
As the weeks progressed, the students who consistently followed the exercise began to really get fervent and personal
as to the things they thanked God for. He began to touch
them deeply. This propelled the students into a place where
they sincerely worshiped God.

Try it. Pray, and then look for the many things you can
praise God for daily. Talk to him about them. An attitude of
praise and worship can truly transform your daily activities.
This attitude can only be sincerely developed through acknowledging God personally in your daily schedule. Some will
say they find it hard to see all the things God does for them.
Begin by getting up in the morning and thanking him for
being alive, because his mercies are new every morning.

It is our job to seek him fervently as if it all depends on
us but to trust him fervently as if it all depends on him. God
is not lost; thus, when I say, "Seek him," a divine principle
is at work. Have you ever noticed God is an if/then God?
"If you are willing and obedient, you will eat the best from
the land" (Isa. 1:19). "If thou wilt diligently hearken to [the
LORD's] commandments, I will put none of these diseases
upon thee, which I have brought upon the Egyptians" (Exod.
15:26 KJV). He is always giving us something to do. The
actions he gives us to do engage our faith, and we know
without faith it is impossible to please God. Our faith, or
action, demonstrates we fully believe God. Our faith is
engaged when we labor for something promised us.

David understood this principle when he numbered the
people and was punished and Araunah offered to give his
cattle for a burnt offering. David replied, "I will not sacrifice
to the LORD my God burnt offerings that cost me nothing"

(2 Sam. 24:24). We have to give God our all if we want his all. God wants us to ask the impossible of him so he can ask the impossible of us. He is bidding you to come closer to him. He stretches out his hand to meet yours, but you must take a step.

Our actions engage our faith. When Jesus came to Lazarus's tomb, he told them to roll away the stone, and he would raise the dead. I have every confidence that if Jesus had told the stone to get out of his way, it would have moved. But he didn't do that; instead, he gave the people something to do, and then he performed the miracle. Why do I say this? Simply because the Lord may require you to do something to engage your faith. Funny; he does that a lot with us. God isn't like a fairy godmother granting our every wish; instead, he uses our desires to grow us up. It is in asking and seeking him that we grow in character and become more like him. It's the little things we do as moms that conform us to his image.

I'm not talking weird stuff here, but simple things, like making a decision to have a ten-minute quiet time daily, or fasting from telephone, television, or computer time. And like Mary, the mother of Jesus, said at the wedding when he performed his first New Testament recorded miracle, "Whatever He says to you, do it" (John 2:5 NKJV)! There are blessings in obedience. It's often a challenge for us to take those little steps because we don't see how they will make a difference in our lives over the long haul, but they do. He is right there with us in the midst of our seemingly mediocre morning routine.

I Will Always Remember You

Let's look again at the last part of 2 Chronicles 15:2. It's a hard pill to swallow, but there it is in black and white. If you forsake the Lord, he will forsake you. He doesn't want to forsake us, but we must not turn away from him. We turn when we give our attention and affection to other things. For instance, when you have a negative attitude or refuse to be thankful, you close your eyes to him.

Ungratefulness is a character trait that will keep us from seeing God, because he is always blessing us. We could never count all our blessings, as the song goes. Being ungrateful may indicate a broader spiritual problem.

We have to keep our eyes on the Lord. We tend to desire what we direct our attention to. So if we want more of God, we have to focus on him in our daily lives. We must not forsake him. I'm sure that's not the case for the majority of us, but I would be remiss if I didn't mention it.

Once we are aware of him, we can clearly see the hand of God, especially as we become determined to seek him diligently. Seek him with all your heart. Cry out to him when you are up at night nursing the baby. Talk to him when your toddler is asking for juice for the fifteenth time. Talk to him when your teenager grows distant and no longer wants to have anything to do with you. Keep pressing in to acknowledge him. Seek him so he can be found. He rewards the diligent. As you do this, you will begin to see him even more in the small details of your day.

Praying Always in All Ways

First Thessalonians 5:17 exhorts us to pray without ceasing. And Luke 18:1–8 likewise says to persist in praying. For years I considered these Scriptures poetic euphemism and not to be taken seriously—especially not by a busy mom. But these Scriptures are indeed possible. I call it the habit of prayer. It's a posture where we continually direct our hearts to God.

This posture is constant conversation with our Creator. When your child does something good, or funny, or inspiring, do you talk to God about it first? Or do you pick up the telephone and call Grandma and Daddy? You should call them, but first you should engage in a dialogue with God. Let him delight in the moment with you.

Having a dialogue with God without knowing his language can be difficult. We need to understand the language of Scripture. The great thing about learning this language is that God himself is our teacher. When we open our Bibles, we can ask him to lead us in Bible study and devotional reading. We can prayerfully ask him what Scriptures we should be memorizing, for the Alpha and Omega knows which ones he will have to bring back to our remembrance.

We have to act in faith. Moms, he is just asking us to open the Bible. It is simple: just open your Bible. You may stash Bibles all around your house, so when you get a moment—or more likely when you take a moment—the Creator of the universe can speak to you. Bibles are so inexpensive, and you can probably get a quantity discount by ordering through the American Bible Society. Put them in the car, the diaper bag, anywhere you go. Get serious for God.

Draw near to him, and he will draw near to you. Be ready to repent. Brother Lawrence said his practice of continually talking with God throughout the day and seeking his forgiveness when he strayed was what made the presence of God come to him easily. It may be a challenge for some to press into the presence of God in our daily activities, but it gets easy as we practice.

Scripture tells us we grow "by constant use" (Heb. 5:14). It will take discipline and a lot of grace to press in, but the benefits to us, our children, our churches, and others are worth it all. We do not have to take big steps. God is

Advice for Practicing the Presence of God

God does not ask much of us. But remembering Him, praising Him, asking for His grace, offering Him your troubles, or thanking Him for what He has given you will console you all the time . . . lift up your heart. . . . Little remembrances please Him.

Everyone is capable of these intimate conversations with God, some more, some less, and God knows what we can do.

I know that for the right practice the heart must be empty of all other things; because God will possess the heart alone; and as He cannot possess it alone, without emptying it of all else besides, so neither can He act there, and do in it what He pleases, unless it be left vacant to Him.

We should establish ourselves in a sense of God's presence by continually conversing with Him. It is a shameful thing to quit His conversation to think of trifles and fooleries.

Let us think often that our only business in this life is to please God. Perhaps all besides is but folly and vanity.

Brother Lawrence, *The Practice of the Presence of God*

concerned more with our consistency. He wants long-term change for us.

There are three critical steps we must take every day. First, ask God what he wants you to do today, and be ready to do it. Second, give thought and planning to long-term things he tells you to do. Third, ask God how he wants you to do what he has asked you to do. Sometimes we get a word from God and think we have to accomplish it in our own strength.

Remember, God rewards those who persistently seek him. We have to be tenacious enough to press in no matter what our schedule may be, and we have to do it now. I have learned that when God speaks, I have to do it immediately; if he tells me to do something I am unable to do immediately—like call a friend—I have to determine in my mind I will do it and not revisit the decision.

It has to become an established fact that I will do it. I find if I wait too long, I will rationalize myself out of things the Lord has told me to do, or the enemy will send someone to discourage me. Therefore, do not wait for an opportune time to be aware of God's presence. Start right now. You made a decision to seek the Lord; do not be moved.

Housework is boring—changing diapers, helping with the schoolwork—it's all rather mundane. Could it be possible that God is in all that? Yes, he is! God wants us to experience his grace in our daily lives. As moms, we can consecrate our days to him and watch him breathe new life into our ordinary day.

God tells us to do everything in the name of Jesus Christ. Thus, we love our children through the love of God and see God in them. Our attitude toward our work will change as we do it with him and as a sacrament to him. Brother Lawrence was able to do menial work in such a way that he said even when he picked up something off the floor, he was aware of God.

Like Brother Lawrence, we too can learn to apply the discipline of prayer to our daily lives. Colossians 4:12 connects praying fervently with staying in the will of God. As moms, we may not always get to spend great amounts of time in prayer, but we can pray fervently or with intensity. We can pray frequently, increasing how often we pray; and we can increase the time we spend in prayer. We can pray with intensity. We can pray frequently, and we can pray at all times. This makes it a habit.

Be real with God. Tell him when you are tired, discouraged, upset, or edgy and, likewise, when you are happy, pleased, excited, or surprised. You cannot hide from God, and he knows anyway.

Where We *Really* Put Our Trust

God knows our circumstances and deals with each of us personally as he transforms us and we become more like him. Therefore, it is important to understand that all the counsel in this chapter should not be used legalistically. It can be overwhelming to you and put a wedge between you and your Creator. More than anything else, God loves you and wants to love others through you. So ask him personally what he wants from you.

Wait on him. He is well pleased with you. Often moms feel like they can never measure up. But God does not want you to measure up; he wants you to die some more so he can be the stronger in you. Commit your time to God and your mind to God. Jesus said to love the Lord God with all your mind, soul, and strength. This means many things for many people, but for you it may mean making slight adjustments so he can do very big things in your life. Let God love through you.

He loves you just as you are. "Come, pull up a chair. Sit down. Let's talk," he says. Listen. Do you hear what he's saying to you?

Prayer

Lord, help me to give my day to you.

7

Follow the Leader

Playing "Mommy Says" on the Mountain

Reading this book may well be like a mountaintop experience. You organize your home, post Scripture, manage to carve out a bit of quiet time, and confidently float into the presence of God. It all seems so grand. Just you and God—if only that were true.

One day after your quiet time, as you gaze at your sculpture of praying hands, you hear the escalating voices: "I did not." "You did too." "No, you hit me first." "No, you hit me." And you realize you're not on a mountaintop anymore. You are still home with your five children, and things really haven't changed much. In fact, they may even be worse.

Moses Comes Down the Mountain

Moses faced a similar dilemma. Here he was on the mountain speaking to God face-to-face and probably interceding for the people who did not want to come near. Put yourself in his shoes. Moses is walking down the mountain with the precious tablets of God in hand. God was going to enter an ever holier covenant with Israel.

God loved Israel so much that he was sending Moses with the tablets of his law. God wanted to know them personally. He wanted to speak with Israel; but when they feared coming near, he gave them his laws, presumably so they could know what he required and begin to understand his love for them. One day, he hoped he would write the law on their hearts, and it would not be an abstract thing. But for now, he had spoken to Moses and given him the task of delivering the tablets to the children of Israel, and so he did.

As Moses walked down the mountain, encased in his arms was God's holy Word; and as far as we know, it was God's first written word to humanity. Moses wrote the first five books of the law, and it appears that up to this point the laws and oracles of God were passed down orally. Imagine God's first written communication with us in our language. Moses, fresh with the glory of God upon him, walks down that mountain. As he grows near, he hears some noise. It sounds like a party, but he senses lasciviousness in the air. Still he walks on, meditating on his forty days on the mountain.

He walks thinking about the great future of these former slaves. He walks holding a revelation of God in his hands. He walks thinking about God's love for the children of Israel. He walks thinking about the lives of his forefathers Abraham, Isaac, and Jacob. He walks knowing these tablets would mark a turning point in the children of Israel's history. They would finally see that they were a holy people separated unto God. He walks with expectancy that God is poised to do a major work for the nation of Israel.

As Moses nears the camp of the Israelites, the noise gets louder and louder; and as he gazes at the camp, he sees the golden calf. The realization hits him: the people have created a self-made image of God. The commandments written on tablets represented God's nature and character as well as his desire for his holy people to live pure and powerful lives. *They* are to be made in *his* image. In hurt, anger, frustration, and betrayal, Moses casts down the precious tablets. *What's the use?* he thinks, furious with the very people for whom he had once interceded. Moses went from the mountaintop and came down into the valley.

The glory of God was all over Moses, yet Moses gave in to anger and cast down God's Word. Moses—yes, Moses—cast down God's Word. The very thing he was angry at the children of Israel about, he did himself. Moses was angry at the people for casting away God's words, but that's exactly what he did when he dropped the tablets. Later, God would reprimand Moses, the very man who had prayed on Israel's behalf. God was ready to raise up a whole new nation; Moses implored God to have mercy; and then God gets angry with Moses for casting down the tablets. Interesting, isn't it?

There are times in our journey to press on to know God more that we have been like Moses too. We get a bit of quiet time in here and there, manage to meditate on a few posted Scriptures, and listen to a good tape. Then we step out of the manifest presence of God, and the glory may still be upon us, but we get angry with our children, and in anger or frustration we do not show forth the glory of God.

Coming Down from Our Mountain

You may be having quiet time in the morning and hear a muted gag. You realize one of the kids has thrown up—right when you are in the middle of communing with God. Jesus understands. His quiet time was interrupted. In Mark 1:35–38, he was disturbed by Simon and the others looking for him. They never said (or at least Scripture does not record them saying), "Sorry for interrupting you." Instead, they said, "Where were you when all the people were looking for you?" Consumed with their own needs and wants, they could not understand why Jesus would even be alone and not available to them. Jesus really understands mothers.

We, as mothers, need to be like Jesus with our children. He did not rebuke them. He got up and went with them, probably realizing only the process of time would change them. We moms must realize only the process of time will change our children; and more importantly, our children are used of God to change us too.

Moses may have had mixed feelings when he was asking God to be merciful to the children of Israel (Exod. 32:11–14). It is interesting to note that God pointed out to Moses what was going on in the camp. God knew exactly what was going on. He saw the Israelites' hearts and knew what they were capable of doing. He may have watched even as Moses implored him to be merciful. It was not until Moses actually saw their outrageous sin for himself that he dropped the tablets. God had already told him what the people were doing. Yet in all this Moses learned a worthy lesson.

God deals with Moses's reaction to the sin of the people and the disobedience of the children of Israel at the same time. God instructs Moses to return to the original process whereby the first tablets were inscribed. God had the power to wave his hand and cause the tablets to be restored to their original condition, but he chose to make Moses go through the process again. It was a lesson for Moses, as well as for the children of Israel. Remember that the next time you come out of your quiet time and are exasperated by your children. God is teaching you both something in the process.

Oh, to Be Like Those Faithful Mothers of Old

So we want to pursue God with all our hearts and minister to our children too. This is a biblical imperative. We have scriptural precedent of godly mothers who have done just that. Mary, the mother of Jesus, comes to mind first. She was a woman God entrusted with his Son.

She was a woman who had grave revelation. But on more than one occasion, Scripture says that after a manifestation of the supernatural or a fulfillment of prophecy or some unusual occurrence validating that Jesus was the Son of God, she "treasured all these things in her heart" (Luke 2:52). She did not call her friends and say, "Guess what, the Savior of the world is in my womb"; nor is there any indication that she belabored the point of his miraculous conception after his birth. She was a mom who knew how to hold her tongue, and she demonstrated a powerful paradigm for us as moms. Some things are between us and God.

God rewards things done in secret that only he sees. We often like to be seen and to be appreciated for our clever words, biblical insight, and scriptural prowess. I struggle with being so candid in my zeal for people to understand and apply the Word of God that I have rashly shared something that God was doing in my character that was just between me and God.

At other times, I have repeated a story, usually of something good I've done, when I saw it impressed people. I know this is wrong. For me building myself up this way is a combination of pride and failure to discipline my tongue. I want people to think well of me. I want to be liked. But in our service to our children or anyone else, we must first serve an audience of one. We must be more concerned about what God thinks first and foremost.

Hannah understood the concept of loving God and serving him through her child. She was a mom sold out to God, who did not live through her child but fully gave Samuel over to the Lord's service. She secured his future by letting go of him even before the umbilical cord was cut. We too, as moms, must nurture our children spiritually so they can hear God for themselves.

Samuel was able to hear God. True, he lived in Eli's house; but Eli had failed to train his own children, and Hannah, in her sacrificial gift back to God, gave Israel a prophet whom God touched so that his words never dropped to the ground. Oh, that we would raise children not to receive the inheritance of sinners (Eli's sons) but to speak to a nation with power. Hannah and Elkanah raised Samuel not in their image but in the image of God.

Samson's mother was also a godly woman who received direct instructions on how to raise her son, including the special diet of a Nazarite. She gave him counsel on what to do; and Samson, like our children, sometimes did not take his parents' advice. Still, she persevered.

Scripture is full of moms who gave a spiritual heritage to their children. Paul speaks of the influence of Timothy's mother and grandmother on him. Although Israel's scribes were part of a primarily patriarchal society, in the books of 1 and 2 Kings, all the kings' mothers are listed as well as their fathers, indicating the mothers too influenced their sons. There is a biblical record of the influence of moms on their children. This should not surprise us.

The Power and Purpose of a Mom

There is significant research that indicates the influence of a mother. In fact, moms have received a lot of backlash from improper toilet training, correction, and so on as a result. In the secular media, you name something that has gone wrong for a child psychologically, and moms are to blame. These days, with the growth of the fathering movement, I understand dads are being blamed as well. However, the Christian mom is often hailed as a paragon of virtue, and those of us who struggle with consistency, patience, and the like may feel ostracized. We should not judge our worth based on someone else's accomplishments.

All of us are being conformed to God's image and struggle with the same things as everyone else. Often we struggle in silence, not wanting anyone to know that sometimes when we are on the mountaintop, like Moses, our children are sculpting golden calves. They are fighting among themselves, growing more selfish, and empowering their flesh. So what are we to do? Well, unlike the children of Israel, our children do not have a choice. They must go up Mount Horeb with us. Am I serious? Yes, I am!

"As for me and my household, we will serve the LORD" (Josh. 24:15). Part of the problem is the way we have treated children in the church. They have been entertained and not made to feel they have a real inheritance in God. Usually by the time our children are teenagers, we notice this and pump time, money, and effort into our youth programs. For most people, youth ministry means teenagers. Even churches that have a children's ministry tend to view it as a prelude to youth ministry and not a vibrant ministry in and of itself. So, moms, you will be climbing a steep mountain as you go against the tide of traditional mainstream Christianity, which has sidelined our children.

How to Choose an Appropriate Bible for Your Child

Generally, toddlers need Bible board books just so they can get used to owning a Bible and using it like the rest of the family. By the time children can recognize a few words or letters, they should have a picture Bible. Choose one with bright pictures and a few words on the pages. Some Bibles even have the Dolch list (words generally used by early readers).

Once your children are at least eight or reading fluently, they will enjoy the New International Reader's Version (NIrV). It's a simplified version of the New International Version.

When choosing a teen Bible, be careful, because some of the extraneous topics in teen Bibles may not necessarily be appropriate for young teenagers (ages thirteen to fifteen). Often young ladies may prefer a very pretty women's Bible instead of a teen Bible. Likewise, young men may prefer an adult male Bible. Derek and I have found our son really prefers a men's Bible as he matures. We have found that by getting separate teen devotionals, young people are more apt to read the Bible and the devotional.

Each time we purchased a different version of the Bible for our children or they moved up in reading or comprehension ability, we made a big deal out of it. We allowed them to go to the Christian bookstore and choose a Bible. Generally we had preselected an assortment of appropriate Bibles (in our price range). Then children feel like owning a Bible is a big deal, and they are also apt to take care of their Bible.

Once I was invited to a prayer meeting for mothers. In fact, we were encouraged to bring our children. As it turned out, Derek had already made plans to do something with the kids, and so blessedly they did not accompany me to the meeting that afternoon. Inwardly, I was excited to be attending a prayer meeting that actually would include the kids. When I got there I noticed all the children were downstairs. Since I had no children with me when I arrived, I did not go downstairs where the children were instructed to go. When the meeting was over, I curiously went downstairs where the children—some as young as two—were assembled, expecting to see someone at least engaging the children in some spiritual discipline. Although I would have preferred them being upstairs praying along with us, I accepted that perhaps they were being guided in prayer or some activity downstairs. Instead, a horror teen flick, with language and graphic sexual innuendos, was playing.

Many of the smaller children were, surprisingly, wrestling somewhat quietly on the floor, and I noticed the empty junk food bags that had obviously been used to bribe them into silence. When I voiced my concern, along with the other moms, the embarrassed hostess did apologize but then added, almost to excuse the whole matter, "Well, at least they were quiet when we were praying." She vowed next time she would choose another video more suitable for children. Later she confided to us that her daughter had been paid to keep the kids "quiet" and that the teen, in obvious rebellion against her mom, had put on the inappropriate video.

I never attended subsequent prayer meetings on several accounts. First of all, the children should have been included in our praying. Second, we should carefully guard who we allow to have influence over our children. This mom knew her child was in rebellion yet gave her authority over innocent children. I found her attitude troubling. Children's ministry is often the hardest place to get volunteers because it is not seen as a viable ministry in some churches. In fact, in many churches background checks are not even done on those who work with our children, and it's the church's dirty little secret that many children are sexually abused by those they have grown to trust in leadership positions. Third, it was not a family prayer meeting to just occupy the children so the mothers could pray. In this particular instance, what bothered me most was that we were praying about children, teen rebellion, and family, and yet directly under us in the basement the very things we were praying against were freely operating. It was sickening to me.

Your children can and will go up to Mount Horeb with you. Up until now I have stressed organizing our homes for power and impact, enhancing our homes for spiritual growth, having a quiet time, talking to God face-to-face, and experiencing the presence of God; but none of these things matter if you cannot take your children with you. It is God's original plan that children would be born into families with both a mom and a dad, and that those children would be mentored into Christianity. Christianity is all about a relationship with God. Love your children, and they will grow to love the God you love. It is our Christian duty to mentor them to maturity.

Unfortunately, many parents in the church treat children as if they are excess baggage. They feel called to do something—anything—even serve on Sunday; and their children get lost in the hustle and bustle of their perceived service to the Lord. God never meant for it to be that way. In fact, many churches are simply reparenting adults who were not given affirmation, approval, and emotional training as children. Most serious emotional issues are childhood scars.

This is not to suggest that children from Christian homes are perfect, because we all deal with issues; but wouldn't you rather learn how to control your tongue at seven than at forty-seven? Think of all the hurt and harm you could save yourself and others if you knew God loved you and you didn't have to seek the love and approval of man. Think of the great works of God that could go forth if we were not encumbered with childish egos and tantrums. I know people are flesh and will sin, but what I am talking about is simple childishness in adults in ministries, which often harms everyone, including the one who does the injuring.

So many issues can be dealt with in child-hood. You know you are a different person today than you were years ago (even if you are a Christian) as a result of learning about God's grace, yielding yourself to him, and

God is a generational God.

being obedient—all simple childlike qualities that will make for a lifetime of success. Are you ready to take your children up Mount Horeb with you? We'll need some essential supplies for the trip.

Going Up to Mount Horeb

Mary's spiritual discernment, Hannah's unselfishness to the plans and purposes of God, and Samson's mother's willingness to raise her son in God's tradition reveal a key principle: just as a mom's primary need is spiritual, so our children need spiritual nurture; and we owe it to them to see that this is not sloppy, haphazard spiritual growth, because they are our gifts from the Lord. Over and over in Scripture, we are reminded that God is a generational God and cares for children deeply. The first thing we will need is a shift in our thinking. Our children desire spiritual growth just as much as we do. They may not be able to articulate it as well as we can, but they need God.

Jesus took time to be with children. He knew the games they played and likened entering the kingdom of God to becoming like a little child. God has given us a window of opportunity into the hearts and minds of our children, and we should not let church service or ignorance get in the way of mentoring them. Jesus taught the crowds but regularly drew himself away to talk to the disciples. The disciples learned everything that Jesus said and did, and he never contradicted his message. His life was his message.

137

> **Jesus took time to be with children. He knew the games they played and likened entering the kingdom of God to becoming like a little child.**

Your life should be a message to your children. Your children's concept of reality rests with you. Even battered and abused children love their parents and, when questioned, will often point to them as pinnacles of love and understanding. Ask God to help you love your children. "But I do love my children," you say. None of us truly loves from a pure heart. We brag on our children, often subverting our own pride. Other times, we find our identity in them.

We often do not realize how much we find our identity in our children. Sometimes I want to look good to others, so I define myself in my children. It is not something I consciously do, but it is an attitude I must guard against. Traveling through those years of infertility, I learned to ask myself some hard questions, like why I really wanted children. I have to admit, my true reasons were not always as noble or Christian as I had hoped they would be. Eventually, I did get to the point that I truly released it all to God and in the process saw Jesus resurrect a real understanding that my children are gifts from him. I can take no credit for them, and I have learned to be real with them.

The other essential tool you will need is a willingness to admit your failures and an ability to apologize to your child. I truly cherish my children and have interceded on their behalf; yet there have been times when I, like Moses, in anger, exasperation, or tiredness, have cast down something precious the Lord had for them. I have to recognize this as sin in my life so I can go back to Mount Horeb and get what God has for them. I am painfully aware that, unlike Jesus, I make mistakes and need to repent to him and my children.

Your children will follow you because they are wired to when they are little. As they get older, they will follow you

138

based on relationship. They need to know you love them. If you tell them you love them with your words but do not express it in deeds, you are confusing them.

Psychologically, a child who has been told one thing with words but shown another with actions and emotions will become a classic neurotic case study. These children do not know whether they should trust their true feelings and emotions—the truth they feel and know—or your self-denial, the lie. These juxtapositions hinder your children's emotional development. You cannot tell your children you love them while talking on the telephone or watching television and expect them to believe it. First, you must pay attention to them and communicate the truth that they are important to you.

I have seen parents ask the church to pray for a wayward child but not go to the Lord themselves on behalf of the child. Often it's easier to cry in front of the church than to intercede and change our behavior toward a rebellious child. I am not discounting a child's freedom of choice or blaming parents who did all they could yet couldn't prevent their child from going astray. I am simply suggesting we go to God first and determine what the problem really is.

Samson's parents followed all the directions of the Lord. He was an insistent—some scholars say spoiled—child who always wanted his way. There came a time when he was released from his parents' covering, and he reaped the consequences of his wrong decisions. But over and over I talk with parents who have young children who aren't being corrected, nurtured, loved, or disciplined. So we have to make a quality decision as we pursue the Lord to diligently go to the Lord on behalf of our children as well.

You will never go to God for help until you recognize the need. It's not surprising that those of us who get lots of grace are the ones who recognize the need. We should constantly be drawn back to God for the strength, grace,

Family Spiritual Growth Tips

- Regularly share what you are reading with other family members.
- We read the Proverbs in the morning. Since there are thirty-one chapters, we follow one chapter for each day of the month. Of course, on shorter months we will miss those later chapters, but since we are constantly rereading, missing a few chapters in any given month is inconsequential. Our little ones may choose what verse in the daily reading they want to read in their own translation. We discuss the Scripture over dinner or during our homeschool family chapel.
- Post a family Scripture for everyone to read and meditate on. We have found posting Scripture in the kitchen works best for us because it is a room we frequent.
- Put times in your schedule to specifically pray with your child. This should occur after your own quiet time, or you will find yourself being frustrated with your child because you cannot have your own prayer time.

and ability to love and disciple our children. Therein is the basis of this book: serving our children should not draw us away from God but should draw us closer to God.

Our daily surrender to the Lord is our road map up Mount Horeb. As our children see us repent, they will likewise learn to repent and come to the Lord. Most importantly, children who learn early to repent and have holy hearts for God see him clearly. Their pureness helps them see him. Scripture tells us that only the pure in heart will see God (Matt. 5:8).

We give our children a precious inheritance. God gave Abraham himself. Abraham was able to give the gift of relationship with God to Isaac, who passed it on to Jacob. God wants to give our children a rich eternal relationship with him. He wants to teach them to serve him. God wants their worship, not because he is egotistical but because he can inhabit the praises of his people.

God is near us when we praise him because we acknowledge him and welcome him into our day. This is not to suggest that God is not near us when we are not praising him, but it is clear that God values a good attitude. The children of Israel roamed forty years in the desert for what could have been a two-week trip because they constantly murmured and complained. I can't help but wonder whether, if they would have stopped to praise God and show their appreciation, perhaps their attitudes would have been changed. In my own life I have found it impossible to complain and praise at the same time. The two are antithetical to one another. When we praise God, it fosters in us an attitude of gratefulness. Therefore, we must praise and worship God as we go up to the place of God. Our children are our disciples, but at the same time they are our brothers and sisters in Christ.

Our children need their own experiences with God. As we go up Mount Horeb, we will need constraint not to step in and guide our children when God wants to guide them. We are to assist the Holy Spirit and not be the Holy Spirit in our children's lives. We must let God convict them, because godly repentance leads to transformation.

This can only occur if, like Mary, we prayerfully and carefully discern the hand of God in their lives and, like Hannah, we let go and trust God to do the work in them. We need to pray and ask God to help us, because as moms, especially godly moms, it is our natural inclination to shelter our children.

We will need fortitude as we go up Mount Horeb. Jesus's disciples were often whiny, jealous of one another, and fighting among themselves. What did Jesus do? He never got in the middle of the arguments about who was right or wrong. He diverted their attention to a more important

This is the secret to effective evangelism—parents on fire for God who can impart their passion and enthusiasm to their children.

issue, much like moms will distract toddlers from the candy strategically placed at their eye level at the supermarket register.

We have to have a higher view to take our children up to Mount Horeb. I am often amazed at the arguments my kids get into with each other right before family vacation or a special treat. I have to reorient them to the bigger issues at hand and not be drawn into their pettiness. Yes, as parents we should give them communication skills, but we also have to constantly tell them about the promises of seeing God face-to-face.

Children are shortsighted. We need the gift of vision for them. We need to cry out and ask God to impart vision. Derek and I have studied the Recabites, descendants of Jonadab, who remained true to their father's traditions even when all of Israel turned away from God. Jonadab imparted to his descendants a zeal for the Lord. Excitement and passion for God really can be passed on to your children.

If you read Jeremiah 35, you will see that the prophet Jeremiah goes to the house of Recab, whose descendants chose to follow their father's precepts concerning the temple and strong drink and other lifestyle choices. The Recabites esteemed their father's words over the prophet's, and God was well pleased with them. God thus promises that they will always have a man stand before God (see Jeremiah 35:18–19). The basis of God making that promise was specifically that they obeyed their father. What a revelation!

Therein is the secret to effective evangelism—parents on fire for God who can impart their passion and enthusiasm to their children. That's why God was called the God of Abraham, Isaac, and Jacob. Each had a revelation with the Lord, but each successive generation received a greater anointing, piggybacking on the previous generation's promises.

Most importantly, we must not find our identity in our children's trek up Mount Horeb. I once heard Tony Campolo say we parents take far too much credit when our kids turn out well and far too much blame when they do not. Christian moms have to be careful not to transgress their relationship with God by validating their mothering skills or identity by how their children turn out or are turning out. This is a trick of the enemy to get even faithful moms to take their eyes off the Lord at the top of Mount Horeb and become encumbered with the process of the climb.

Even children raised in the same home are different temperamentally and emotionally. Thus we cannot control how our children react to things that happen to them. For instance, it's documented that some children of alcoholics become alcoholics and others become overly responsible. I am oversimplifying here just to make a point, but why does this occur? It has more to do with individual responses to stimuli than anything else. Some children in godly homes serve the Lord faithfully, others leave the fold and never return, and some stray for a while only to return after a time. If we get too caught up in what we did right or wrong as parents, we make ourselves a god. Someone once pointed out to me that in Scripture even Moses's children were swayed wrongly by the crowd. It is our job to teach our children to climb, and it is God's job to meet them there.

Keys to Draw Close to God

There are three keys to teaching your children to draw close to God. First, impress upon them that God wants to be close to them, just as they want to be close to him. Second, tell them he cannot be found in a method. Methods should motivate them to seek God for themselves. Methods minimize God, as over time people begin to rely on the methods instead of their relationship with God. Also, when we put God in a method box, we do not have to change. Third, teach your children to pray and read the Bible daily and to fellowship with believers. But these methods of growing should never replace God himself.

God is not impressed with what we do. He is impressed with the condition of our hearts. Our actions may appear good, but God weighs the motives. Throughout the Bible, God commands his people to have pure hearts. Even Jesus continually urged people to get their hearts right. John the Baptist's whole ministry was to prepare people's hearts so they could know God. If we want to be close to God, we must lay our hearts on the altar. The altar is the place of exchange where God can cleanse us.

Most times we cannot see our heart's true intent. It is camouflaged by pride, sin, religion, past hurts, and misconceptions. Therefore, we must daily place our hearts on the altar of God's Word and willingly allow his Spirit to purify our hearts. The purification process must be initiated by the Holy Spirit, lest we become too introspective and fall into condemnation as opposed to Holy Spirit conviction. If we try to do it on our own, we just feel guilty when we don't measure up. However, if God does a work in our hearts, he energizes us because it is all part of the process of being more like Christ. If we try to do it on our own, even if we are successful, we fall into the grip of pride.

Pride is an ever-present reality in our hearts. I often have to check myself because pride is so insidious. It often masks itself as wanting to be right, and it's fortified in hollow religious duty. One Sunday a sister asked me a question regarding her child's schooling. It was obvious, to me anyway, that she was really looking for validation of a wrong

More Spiritual Growth Tips

- Choose a Bible storybook to read to your child so that he or she can get a broad understanding of the Bible.
- Pray for your child. Pray with your child.
- Let your child observe your prayer posture. Children learn by example. Allow them to occasionally sit quietly nearby while you pray or have your quiet time.

decision she'd made. I matter-of-factly pointed out what I perceived to be "the truth." (Christian translation of "the truth"—your opinion cloaked in self-righteous religious jargon, occasionally combined with a few out-of-context Bible verses to strengthen your pride.)

When I walked away from her, I felt a bit uneasy. I tried to shake the feeling. After all, I rationalized, I told her the truth. In this case what I said was legally, morally, and ethically correct, plus I had said it in love (or so I thought). I was correct in my assessment of the problem, I reasoned. Still, the Holy Spirit gently said to me, "Cheryl, do you want to be right, or do you want to help her?"

I repented. My pride had been more concerned about being right than being "my brother's keeper." As I prayed, the Spirit spoke to my heart. Immediately, I called her. I did not say, "God told me to tell you this." Instead, I merely went to her in love and repented for not listening more closely. As a result, the situation completely turned around. Her child was helped, and she drew close to God. In short, God was glorified!

The best thing we can do for our children is to be emotionally whole. We must not be afraid to admit we were wrong, and our children should not carry our emotional baggage. Our own hearts deceive us at times. Even though I wanted to help this sister, it was my pride that motivated me. Don't you see how deceptive our hearts can be and why we need a Savior?

Share your successes and failures with your child so he or she can grow. Be mindful of your child's age, and do not grieve your child with your struggles. Simply share when you triumph over sin, and please do not be so specific about the sin that the sin is magnified over God himself.

Teach your children to read the Bible with the eyes of the Spirit—with God talking to them and instructing them as they read. Nurture an expectancy that God can and does speak through his Word. Allow them to be educated by the Holy Spirit. Teach them to read God's Word with joy, not drudgery. Teach them to read complete books of the Bible in context. Cults and even Satan himself use the Word of God out of context. Encourage them to ask God to lead them in their Bible study. Explain to them that Bible study is interactive and that it's okay to ask God questions and to clarify as they read.

Entering into the Holy of Holies with Your Child

The Old Testament tabernacle represented heaven in all its splendor. The colors, materials, and workmanship of the tabernacle all testified to the glory of God—it was his dwelling place! The tabernacle was the place where the children of Israel met God. Basically, it had three compartments: the outer court, the inner court, and the Holy of Holies, or Most Holy Place. The Holy of Holies was where the very presence of God rested. Only the high priest entered the Most Holy Place, once a year on the Day of Atonement to make sacrifices for the sins of the people that year. As a result of Jesus's sacrifice, we may freely enter the Most Holy Place. He is our high priest. Now we enter the Holy of Holies for ourselves.

146

Our children must enter the Holy of Holies with us. God is a generational God. He is the God of Abraham, Isaac, and Jacob. He has promised us and our children a relationship. The greatest gift God can give anyone is himself. God showed favor to Isaac and Jacob, Abraham's descendants, based solely on his relationship with their forefather. Above anything else, I want my children to have a relationship with God. I know you want that too. Yet sometimes we can get so caught up in ministering to our children's physical and emotional needs that we forget they too must experience God. Their greatest need is to know God for themselves.

Sometimes we can get so caught up in ministering to our children's physical and emotional needs that we forget they too must experience God for themselves.

We must empower our children to daily seek God. They too must have a quiet time, a time to meditate on Scripture, to read the Bible, and to come to a personal knowledge of and a genuine relationship with Jesus Christ. God has no grandchildren. Your children are also your brothers and sisters in the Lord. Nurture a love for the Word of God in them. Get them translations they can understand. The New International Reader's Version is excellent for children. There are also numerous teen devotionals. Choose wisely. Get one that fits the character of your child. Discuss the Scripture with your child frequently. Apply it.

Finally, be ever vigilant that you do not resent serving your children. Ask God to give you a pure attitude toward them. Allow them to grow into who God wants them to be. Pray with them. Pray for them. Yield yourself as a tool God can use in their lives to make a difference for him. Just as Jesus led his disciples even when they annoyed him or seemed not to understand, so you too are called to lead your children, knowing that a great reward awaits you in heaven.

Prayer

Lord, help me to give myself to you so that I can give myself to my family. Amen.

8

Passing the Baton

Let the Children Come—
Allowing the Kids to Join in the Chase

"Going to have any more children?" she asked, giving me a sympathetic look, although at the time I thought it more pathetic than supportive. She motioned to help me, but the awkwardness of the moment was obvious and uncomfortable for both of us.

I shot her a strained look, as I thought it was obvious I wasn't going to answer her question, and I nodded no, thank you, to her offer of help. My indignation was coupled with my embarrassment as I indiscreetly gathered rolling Cheerios that were seeking refuge in the dusty corners of our church lobby, because my daughter had managed to undo her toddler spill-proof lid. Prior to this conversation, the only words I had exchanged with this sister were "Praise the Lord," "Grace and peace," and "Have a blessed week." You know, one of those meaningful conversations in church that really builds community and fosters understanding among the saints. It was also obvious since I saw her every week that either she had no children or her children were grown.

I thought that through my polite silence and the awkwardness of the situation, she might get the hint that I was not going to answer the question. Before I could say something, she blurted out, "I have two." Putting her hand out to offer to toss the dirty Cheerios, she continued, "A boy and a girl, and I'm finished."

"Really," I said. I wanted to say a lot. I'm never at a loss for words, but the Scripture in Proverbs about being thought wise by not answering a fool according to his folly came to my mind. I struggled to think of something to say to end the conversation and maintain my Christian witness. After all, we were just coming out of service. "Are they serving the Lord?"

"No." Surprisingly, she pressed on with little encouragement from me. "You know, they're teenagers, and I've done my job. Sometimes they do come to the youth service. But hey, I did my job. I brought them to church when they were little. Now I'm doing so much in the ministry that I just don't have the time for their dawdling on Sunday morning. If they aren't ready to leave when I'm ready, that's too bad for them. That's why I'm glad I only had two and I spaced them out so they really weren't much of an interruption . . . if you know what I mean."

The truth was, I wasn't sure what she meant, but it was clear her children had not been a priority in her life. It's really sad that many in the church do not value children. Some give lip service to loving children like Jesus did, but church resources and energies are rarely directed to children's ministry. Since children are not valued, neither is mothering. But all mothers have a high and holy calling, because we are to disciple the next generation of Christians.

It is indisputable: God cherishes children. After all, they are his. That is a hard concept for us to get: our children are not really our own. They belong to God. Over and over in Scripture, God calls children his own. He is specifically sharp in Ezekiel 16:20–21, where he rebukes Israel for sac-

> Behold, children are a heritage from the LORD.
>
> Psalm 127:3 NKJV

rificing their sons and daughters. God says, "You took the children you bore to me and sacrificed them to idols."

All our children belong to God. They are not ours. They are his. Therefore, we must get instructions from God as to how to raise our children and trust God to lead us in the process. We must lead our children back to their Creator.

So as we journey up Mount Horeb for direction, some of us feel a little inadequate. After all, we've barely had a full night's sleep, and we haven't spent much time alone with God. Yet we are called to this awesome task. We must bring God back his children. Like Hannah who gave Samuel over to the service of the Lord, all of us Christian moms must give our children back to God.

The Lord bids us come to him and not look at the steepness of the mountain, nor at the tough terrain, nor at the uncertainty of the mountain caves. Just as he did with the children of Israel, he bids us to come up the mountain. So we lead our children to the foot of the cross. We cannot make them accept the Lord, but we can take them to the place where God wants to meet with them. We can teach them to trust God to part the Red Seas in their lives. He is there with us in the pillar of cloud by day, and he guides us up the mountain. We simply have to trust him.

Learning to Trust Him

Trusting God is an active process, because we only trust him to the degree we move. The children of Israel moved with the cloud. They followed faithfully. Trusting God in-

Trusting God is an active process, because we only trust him to the degree we move.

volves moving when he moves and stopping when he stops. Trusting God means we know him. We know he has a good end in mind even if we don't know what that end will be. Our trust in God grows every day as moment by moment we move with the cloud. Like Peter when he walked on the water, we constantly look to Jesus.

If we listen to the voices of the other disciples in the boat, they may distract us and get our eyes off Jesus. It is gazing at him, looking into his loving eyes, and seeing his outstretched hand that gives us the confidence that we can walk on water.

As we discussed in chapter 7, Moses got distracted from his mission to deliver the tablets to the children of Israel; we must not be distracted by the very people we serve. When we hear the voice of God, we must not be distracted by our children. How do our children distract us? They distract us just by being themselves. Children are not like us. Let's face it; we are simply annoyed by their immaturity. We expect them to enjoy the trek up Mount Horeb as much as we do. We just want them to follow us step by step, moment by moment, never veering off course. However, they like to stop, examine the rocks, pick some mountain flowers, drink water from a spring, play with their sister. . . . Really, they just want to enjoy the experience. We just want the experience with no frills.

The Mystery of Childhood

Childhood is such a wonderful mystery to me. Although I've worked in children's ministry for years, been a schoolteacher, and, of course, spent time with my own kids, there is a part of the process of being children I still do not understand. They are so open, honest, and vulnerable. They possess a perception of purity. They question unashamedly. Their concept of time is almost nonexistent. They rapture in the process of things. Little ones taken by the activities of ants will trail them through the backyard the whole afternoon; or little ones who love dinosaurs will read every dinosaur book and go on a bone excavation. I can see why Jesus related the kingdom to little children. I enjoy these qualities about them.

There are qualities I don't like about children too. They are often impatient, demanding, and in a world all their own. They do not see the bigger picture. I think Jesus had to deal with these same qualities in his disciples.

The difference between adult sin and children's sin is that adults have been more socialized to cover it up. You see a sister at church whom you don't like, and you avoid her or put on a plastic smile. You're socialized enough to know scorn is inappropriate. If your son scrunches up his face when he sees another child he had a conflict with, you immediately correct him. You will probably throw in a lecture for good measure because then you'll feel like you've done the parenting thing well. You've corrected a wrong. But have you? No, you have not. You haven't dealt with the issue of his heart. Indeed, what you have taught him is to turn his emotions inward and put on a phony Christian smile like you.

This kind of behavior will hinder his spiritual growth, because God requires pure hearts of all those who come into his presence. Therefore, it is our job not to lecture but to stop and make children aware of their sin, get them to freely acknowledge it, and move them to the process of repentance. This, moms, can be quite a distraction as we rigorously strive to enter the presence of God. Dealing with sin is just part of the calling of motherhood, and the sooner we face it, the more inclined we'll be to deal with it.

Most of us spend our time indiscriminately reacting to behavior we wish wasn't there; others of us spend our time denying behavior we see; and still others of us spend our time modeling children into adults so we can enjoy them. None of these is a godly response. We should be daily seeking God for his plan for our children. The issue is that in our quest to understand children, we adopt philosophies that are not biblical. We become so consumed with "fixing" children that we address *all* parenting situations based on that approach. We assume it will work all the time and every time with all our children.

Why We Do What We Do

Parenting approaches or ways to fix our children are all over the place. It seems everyone is an expert. These different beliefs stem from different views of children, and we have to guard our hearts in this area, because whatever method we embrace will have a long-term effect on our relationship with our children. We must therefore choose prayerfully, understanding that each approach has its own strengths and weaknesses.

One parenting approach believes that children are God's creation, they belong to him, and the world belongs to them. They should live unfettered lives so that they can go explore and find out who they are. They should enjoy childhood and experience all there is to life. They should be dealt with with kindness, understanding, and tremendous restraint, and they should never be corrected with the Bible, as they will come to resent God and his harsh commandments. Your children are self-indulgent and often embarrass you publicly, but you have come to accept that as a badge of motherhood—even though your twelve-year-old still throws tantrums for candy in the supermarket aisle. You look at

Heart–to–Heart Things to Do with Your Child

- Enter the world of your children. It is a great place of wonder. Jesus likened us to little children. Spend some time crawling on your knees to see the world from your children's point of view. Play pretend games with them. You will find yourself refreshed.
- Foster critical thinking in your children by encouraging them to ask why. Preschoolers are naturally inquisitive. Sometimes we squash this in older children by discouraging their questions.
- Writing to your children reveals your heart. We write to our children often, using what I call interactive journals. My kids write letters to Derek and me, and we respond. Sometimes they ask silly questions or things about our childhood, family rules, church traditions, or homeschool lessons, and we answer them. Other times they reveal what they're thinking about a certain topic. The journals are not a substitute for family conversation, but as our children have gotten older, the journals have become a catalyst for initiating sensitive subjects. This is especially true for older children who like to be more secretive and may not blurt out their emotions. Journals have the added bonus of developing their writing and reasoning skills.

those other poor little socialized children knowing that God is on your side, and that makes you feel good.

The second parenting approach believes that children are inherently evil and seek to take your time, your attention, and your very life from you. These parents are encouraged to get a jump on the situation before the baby comes home from the hospital. Children should not be cuddled excessively or allowed to explore the environment. Their sinful nature must be constrained. They will do as you say or else receive the rod of reproof, which God has ordained you to apply to their bottom. If they should ever step out of the parameters you have drawn for them, which are often quite small, they will receive instant and exact punishment. Because of your rules, restraints, and restrictions, they make you look good when you go out because they fear reprisal when they get home. You sneer at others' children knowing you have heard from the throne yourself.

The third parenting approach is rather gruff. After all, "My mama didn't read no parenting books" or adhere to any "approach," and you turned out just fine. In fact, you think people spend too much time discussing what to do with the kids. You just have to deal with them until they are grown up. You spank them occasionally, if they cross your proverbial line, and affirm them when the teacher says they need to be more positive. If they are to learn morality, you'll take them to the youth group on Friday night while you go to the gym. After all, you had a life before you had children, and you will continue after you have children. God didn't just call you to be a mother; in fact, you're a prophet to the nations, and when you go out to minister, you bribe your children to behave so all can see what a great parent you are. You've prayed for them and done your Christian service, or so it seems. Soon they will be grown and out of your home, and you can continue on with your life.

So What Does the Bible Say?

The most insidious thing about a lie is the degree of truth in it. All these approaches have a strain of biblical truth and at one time or another were popular in the body of Christ. Let's look at each. In the first approach children are almost deities, in the second they are demonized, and in the third they are simply dismissed. All of these approaches are wrong. Children are a gift from the Lord and should not be ignored or seen as evil inheritances or seen as God himself. Children are a gift from the Lord. And how would you treat a gift God gave you? Preciously. Tenderly. Wisely. Cautiously.

True, there are elements of God's view in all of these parenting styles. What should you do with your children? Go to God for instruction; and if you have fallen into using any one man's (or woman's) style of parenting, repent. Repent because only God can give you instructions for your child. As parents, we may gather information from the "experts," but ultimately God has given us our children to steward.

Could you imagine Samson's mother listening to the other moms at the marketplace talking to her about how strange Samson looked with long hair? Think about it. Samson's hair was never cut from childhood—it had to be touching his ankles at one point. Can't you just hear them saying, "God understands if you just cut a bit off"? Or what about Samuel? Can't you hear Hannah's friends saying, "But God would understand if you change your mind about giving Samuel up. Besides, he really does not require all that. After all, there is nothing in our law about giving away children"? Mary, the mother of Jesus, could have severely reprimanded him for being in the temple and staying behind. He had to know his parents would be missing him. Was Jesus disobedient? No, he was about his Father's business.

Our children must likewise be about their Father's business. Proverbs 22:6 states, "Train up a child in the way he should go: and when he is old, he will not depart from it" (KJV). Many in the church have used that Scripture to excuse teen rebellion and turning away from the Lord. Most churches have tremendous youth (and by youth I mean teenager) ministries, because most churches identify the teen years as the problem. The truth is, the teen years generally are just a manifestation of the early years. My husband, who has worked with families in crisis for twenty years, tells me he often sees parents trying to parent their troubled teens the way they should have done when they were younger. It is sad to watch this same pattern even in our churches.

The real meaning of Proverbs 22:6 is far more than most of us, including me, understand. The word *train* in the Scripture is from the Hebrew word that means "to dedicate, as in a temple." The Amplified Bible alternately renders "in the way he should go" as "in keeping with his individual gift or bent."

There are many books to help adults find their purpose that have a great emphasis on writing mission and vision statements. Imagine the impact on the world if our children had their own vision and mission statements. "But my child wants to do everything," you reason. Therein is the process of dedication: narrowing down—not totally eliminating, but keying in on—your child's gifts and talents.

This can only occur as you lay your heart before the Lord. We moms must pursue God every day, because we need a fresh revelation of what he wants to do in the lives of our children. Scripture records that Mary was a woman who "treasured all these things in her heart" (Luke 2:51). When she brought Jesus to be circumcised, she listened to the words of Anna the prophetess. She did not ask for the words to be explained to her; rather, she held them in her heart, perhaps pondering them with the Father. As moms, we should hold things in our hearts that the Lord impresses upon us for our children. I write them down in my journal and in a book I have for my children. Actually, I write notes to them frequently in a special book. One day I will give it to them. Perhaps it will be used as a means for God to confirm his Word to them.

Doing It Like Jesus

We should parent our children in much the same way Jesus trained his disciples, in love, understanding, and continuous fellowship with the Father. In reality, our children should spur our spiritual growth, because they are not ours and we need God's directions. Our children are the Lord's. Most of you are sighing, "But I know that already, Cheryl. I recognize that God has called me to minister to my children and that he alone will guide me in the parenting process." I'm glad we agree; but the greater question is, when you say "parenting," what does that word mean to you?

Webster's dictionary describes *parents* as "those who bring forth offspring." But as Christians, what does it mean to parent? It means we come alongside God to grow our children into Christians. Secular parents probably view raising their children as socializing them into citizens of their country's educational, political, and governmental system. As Christian parents, we have a charge to raise our children to proactively and passionately pursue God and his purposes.

The wording makes all the difference in the approach. I find the term *parenting* very vague. I like the term *discipling*—like Jesus did with his followers. His disciples learned how to walk by living with Jesus. Our children likewise will either learn our ways or God's ways. We should be dying, and daily they should see Christ, not us.

Are there some methods that work with sinful hearts? Yes, there are; but even these methods should not be used to the exclusion of a relationship with God or our children. First rely on your relationship with God, and ask him what the real issue may be. A two-year-old with tantrums may be tired. A twelve-year-old with tantrums may be manipulating you. It is imperative that you possess a basic understanding of child development.

Child development is one area that God has showed me I need to understand. While I want my children to imitate me as I imitate Christ, I must also be mindful that I do not push them to do things when they have not reached that developmental milestone. I have learned to listen to that still, small voice in regard to my children, because some issues are not a matter of disobedience but simply a sign that my child needs to mature to be able to sit still longer. I also have to be careful not to compare my children to other children their age. We really need to spend time with God praying for our children before we jump to any conclusions concerning their behavior. I have had to repent many times when I made rash judgments about my children's behavior.

One of the Scriptures the Lord gave me a long time ago was 2 Corinthians 10:6, that I "will be ready to punish every act of disobedience, once [my] obedience is complete." We cannot ask our children to come up higher and be holier than we are and not model godly behavior for them. I am amazed at parents who seem intolerant of their toddler's whining yet in their own adult way whine about every inconvenience; or messy parents who insist their children wake early and make their beds while the parents roll into their unmade beds each night.

We must constantly be transformed. We are living sacrifices and daily must stay on the altar. Please do not be discouraged in this process; repentance should be joyful, because God always promises a reward for repentance. The cutting away of the flesh yields a powerful fruit. God rewards those who diligently press into him. Do you know what your reward will be? More of him! Our children need more of God.

We want to impart to our children the desire to know God better. We want to impart to our children a love for God's Word. We want to impart to our children an eternal relationship with their Creator so that he will be a part of our family forever. That is what every mom wants, isn't it? So deal with the sin in your child's life prayerfully. Go to God about it.

Deal with it intelligently. Read godly, inspired parenting books. Be certain to find out about the author's philosophy and personal life. Pray before you read any parenting book, because the author's philosophy has the ability to influence your child.

Parent Them Now, Not Later

I realize I am coming down rather hard on some things here, but to me being a parent is a tremendous spiritual responsibility. It requires utter maturity. Often, as I have said before, many of our churches are simply reparenting adults, teaching us restraint, reasonableness, and responsibility. These things should have been taught to us as children.

Sacrifice is also a concept not taught in our churches today, but it is a valid biblical principle. One of the qualities of mature people of the faith is their ability to give so that the right hand does not know what the left hand is doing. When we do our good in secret, it is God who rewards us openly. I have found doing the right thing, even when it's hard, builds character when it is just us and God.

There is great spiritual joy to giving without recognition or reward. It's as if there is a secret between us and God. We should not even belabor our children with what God tells us to do, especially in regard to their sin. Does this mean we constantly clean up after them and do not let them know of our to-do list? Of course not. They should learn responsibility, accountability, timeliness, diligence, and the reward of doing a job well. Many adults possess very little of these skills themselves because they were not taught those skills as children. Perhaps their parents thought they would pick them up by osmosis or just never made the time to teach these skills.

Go to the Lord and ask him what skills you need to impart to your children. Sometimes something that may be an irritant to us is not a major issue, and that's why we need to talk to God about it. This is a bit sticky, but we must also have pure hearts toward our children. "Well, of course I have a good attitude toward my child; I love him," you insist. Our motives toward our children are not always pure. We may be annoyed because they bite their nails. While it may not be a good habit to have, the greater issue may be that they remind you of a former boss you hated. This, of course, is on the unconscious level. Or perhaps you think they are scattered, but you have done little to provide structure for them, and looking at them reminds you of your sin. However, rather than repent, you make them the problem. Hard stuff, right?

It's a good practice to go to the Lord before you address any behavior and to ask him to help you look at it objectively. For instance, once I thought one of my children whined a lot. So I made a chart of the actual number of times during the day the child whined, the events preceding it, and the ensuing consequences for the behavior or the events generally following the behavior. I learned I was maximizing a behavior that really did not occur that often. I didn't like the behavior and had maximized it in my own mind. I had to be more tolerant with that phase of child development. Seeking the Lord as you minister to your children is paramount. Do you see why I say parenting is an awesome job?

We must also be careful not to punish children for just being children. This kind of punishment is most damaging to their souls because it strikes at the core of their being. They find their self-definition in our treatment of them.

Children do not process information like, "Mom had a hard day; that's why she yelled at me." They are very tender. They tend to think something is wrong with them.

Three Ways You Can Communicate Love to Your Children

1. Eye contact. Stop what you are doing and look at your children when they talk to you. Paying attention communicates to your child that they are more important than anything else you're doing.
2. Touch. If possible but not artificial, touch your children when they are speaking to you. A light treasuring tap on the shoulder or a stroke on the arm lets your children know you are there for them emotionally too. You hear them, but more importantly, you feel what they are saying. Of course, if your child is really upset, a hug or kiss is more appropriate than a subtle supportive stroke.
3. Positive gestures. Nod that you understand when your children are talking. Gesture with your hands to encourage your children to continue speaking when they pause, because this indicates you are interested. Children, unlike adults, cannot separate their thoughts from themselves. Showing an interest in what they are saying is equated to showing an interest in them. We should resist the temptation to speak by giving affirming nods and positive gestures. Our nonverbal behavior speaks volumes to our children.

Many psychologists point to unhealed childhood wounds as adult neurosis. We have to be careful to minister to our children as God would want us to do. I find I am on the altar a lot in this area. I pray often for God to give me the grace to respond to my children lovingly even when I am stressed or annoyed or when they don't move as quickly as I want them too.

I also have to have realistic expectations of them. Making unreasonable and unrealistic demands frustrates children. For instance, asking a nine-year-old with no inclination for physics to sit still and straight during an intense meteorite lecture, and then scolding the child when he is unable to do so, is unfair and inhumane.

To require a child to do something physically and mentally impossible is abuse. Now if the child was interested in meteorites and wanted to find out all he could, and you were limited in your knowledge of the subject, it would be just and wise to bring him with you to an astronomy lecture. Of course, you should also bring things to occupy him if the subject matter gets too complicated for him to comprehend. It is quite an individual thing. We walk the balance beam, because I am a firm believer in exposing children to things that interest them and stir their curiosity, even if other children are not traditionally included. My children have helped out at homeless shelters, attended university lectures, and participated in adult prayer conferences, all because they showed an interest. You have to seek God for your children and their calling so you can cooperate with the Holy Spirit.

Get to the Heart of the Matter

We must also deal with the sin in our children's lives in a proactive way. We have to teach our children letter sounds before we tell them to sound out a word. It is the same with character development. If we want our children to be patient, kind, and long-suffering, we have to teach them. These days, modeling is just not sufficient, because many of us do not have solid biblical models from our own upbringing. Therefore, as a family you may have to study biblical roles and learn to apply Scripture to real life. For instance, when our family memorized "A soft answer turns away wrath" (Proverbs 15:1 NKJV), we all looked for opportunities to apply the Scripture. And as you know, conflict is part of life, so opportunities were always arising.

The Bible is the best source for teaching. There are also many books available on character training. Character education is important, but we do not naturally gravitate to the good; therefore, we have to teach our children how to make good choices. You do not have to do a long complicated lesson; a simple discussion over breakfast or lunch will do. I realize dads are called to provide spiritual leadership, but moms often spend time putting out fires instead of proactively providing leadership to their children. Once you teach your child the standard when you are dealing with misbehavior, you will be able to reference the correct behavior instead of just pointing out the negative. In that way you are teaching your children how to eventually correct themselves.

What Did You Say?

Listening is a vital life skill that should be taught early. In fact, more of us would benefit from developing our listening skills further. The first step is to be able to repeat the speaker's words with a degree of understanding. Your children should not merely parrot words of others but demonstrate some reflective thought about what has been said. Active listening to parents, peers, and siblings helps children communicate on a deep level that will likewise transfer over to their communication with the Lord. In a nutshell, active listening involves listening to the speaker and reflecting back the speaker's thoughts and feelings to make sure you have understanding. You'll have to model this a few times to children. Here's an example:

Joey: You were late picking me up from baseball. I was the last kid there.

Mom: It must have been pretty scary being all by yourself.

Joey: Yeah. I thought you would never come.

Mom: I'll try harder to be on time next time. I'll ask Jesus to help me. Do you think you can ask Jesus anything, Joey?

Joey: Yes. I can pray when I am alone; after all, Coach Roberts was right there too.

Let's notice some steps this mom took. She did not invalidate Joey's feelings by telling him Coach Roberts was there nor by explaining away her lateness. She acknowledged his feelings and didn't react to his agitation. Being an adult means taking the high road and not expecting our children to make us feel good about our choices. This mom also turned the child back to Jesus and got him to reason on his own. Since he felt validated, he was eventually able to reason he really was not alone. Coach Roberts was right there. Children tend to aggrandize everything, and had Joey not acknowledged Coach Roberts, his distorted view of reality would become commonplace in other, similar areas.

This mom also had to be at a place of peace where she did not react to Joey's accusation. A soft answer turns away wrath. Later, this mom could talk to Joey about how to speak to someone even in crisis. Children should be taught respect even when they are upset, but children, like us, first need to be validated before being corrected.

Practice active listening. It's imperative to show empathy with children when listening. Children still have an element of fantasy in their thoughts, and you can use that to show you want the best for your child, even when you cannot give it. Listen without the temptation to give one of those lectures that often goes in one ear and out the other. Do you remember any childhood lectures? I don't. I do remember how I felt and how angry my parents were. Only by listening and getting to the heart of the issue will you be sure to strike a chord with your child. Here's an example:

Joey: I hate church, and I can't even find my shoes. Why can't we just stay home today?

Mom: I wish I could just say, "Shoes, be here," and they would magically appear, but I can't help you. I have to feed your baby sister.

Joey: But Mom, I left them right here last night. I don't want to wear my sneakers.

Mom: I know you wish the shoes were right there. Church is in five minutes. Please be at the door with something on your feet.

Admittedly this is a serene scenario, but I just wanted to make my point. Again, this mother offers empathy since she is unable to leave the baby to help look for the shoes. She says she wishes they could magically appear. The problem with the shoes isn't immediately solved, but Joey does know Mom cares about him. Mom also does not get in any long conversations. After church would be the time to discuss where to put shoes so they are easy to retrieve.

I don't agree with some secular parenting books that say, "Do not tell the child not to say 'hate.'" Once the child's feelings and frustrations have been validated, his use of the word *hate* and rash thought process should be addressed. Children can learn purposeful thinking too. In fact, the sooner they learn it, the better.

Children need to know they share in the process of decision making and are not blindly obedient. One thing that has worked in our family is that the children will say, "I understand you want to _____ because _____, but I want to make an appeal." For instance, "I understand you want me to finish my math work because we will be going away on the weekend; but may I make an appeal, because I want to finish my computer project, and then I promise to finish my homework this evening."

This opens dialogue, and the children begin to understand not just our acts but our ways. Moses knew God's ways; the children of Israel knew his acts. Acts are arbitrary demonstrations of his power, whereas an understanding of his ways provides us with a profound understanding of why God does what he does. This appeal process helps our children to reason from our adult point of view. It likewise teaches them to see life from our point of view and relate to us, because often they have to provide Scripture when making an appeal. It likewise teaches them to see life from God's point of view and to relate to him. Positional authority is still enforced because the child has to make the request, and we, the parents, oblige ourselves to listen and accept or reject the proposed option.

Our children's needs can draw them, and us, closer to God, as often God is working out something awesome in everyone. As we confess our frustrations to God, he is there to minister to us; and as he speaks to us, we too begin to understand his ways.

What Every Child Needs

Children need to be emotionally secure before we can tell them about the love of God. Children need attention. Stop. Look your children in the eye. Touch them. Even when our children seem to push us away, we need to cuddle them. Our sons might not appreciate a hug, but we can ruffle their hair and give approving touches along with words of affirmation.

I tell my children, "Moms need ten hugs a day"; but, in fact, children need them. They think they're accommodating me, and in a sense they are. I get just as much, perhaps more, out of hugging them. We also have to consciously say positive things to our children. Be real, and ask God to help you—not to just parrot words, but to sincerely believe them. Ask God to give you joy in serving your family so that you may impart joy to them.

Our actions and emotions must match. We cannot tell our children we love them and at the same time be on the telephone when they come in from school. Children remember things emotionally.

Our children need affirmation, approval, affection, and a sense of belonging. These things are essentials in the life of our children. We can only give these to our children to the degree that we love life ourselves. You cannot tell your child what a blessing he or she is unless you are convinced yourself that life is a blessing. Yes, life is serious, but we must find the joy and delight in it so we can play with our children. Jesus played with children. He knew their sing-song games. He had rapport with children.

Children learn most by what we do. We have an intentional plan for our children. It is primarily our responsibility to nurture a love of God in our children so that they hunger after God.

Prayer

Lord, help me to help my child hunger after you.

9

The Right Attitude

Living in the Joy and Grace of the Moment

"We caught your hints, Mommy," my seven-year-old beamed as she placed the gift box in front of me on the floor and my family all surrounded me in anticipation. "Open it."

Smiling, I hoped they had picked up my not-so-subtle hints about getting some nice black ink gel pens, stationery, or planner refills for Christmas. I had really hinted big time for the pens. I especially hated running out of "my" pens. It seemed everyone always used them, and I was the one left borrowing their pens. So more than anything else, I hoped the kids would get me my own black gel pens with comfort grips. They were a bit too pricey for me to buy for myself—not terribly expensive, just slightly more than I was used to spending for pens. Funny, if the kids needed gel pens I would buy them, but I could never bring myself to spend that much money on myself on something that I did not consider a necessity.

Derek and I had always been very practical since we'd had kids and made the decision for me to stay home. We had opted not to exchange gifts for ourselves during the holidays. Instead, our finances were directed toward gifts for the kids and some charitable causes we wanted to support. However, as the kids got older, they insisted on getting gifts for us. We agreed to receive the gifts as long as they were practical and did not exceed a certain dollar limit. The gel pens were well within the price range for the kids to get them for me. So when Jolene placed the box in front of me, I prepared myself to look surprised and pondered where I would hide them so only I could use them.

As I gazed down at the box, it looked rather large for gel pens, but our family was known for throwing suspicious family members off the scent of an anticipated gift by wrapping earrings in a shoe box or stuffing a shirt in a coffee mug. Since the kids seemed overly excited about me opening the gift, as did Derek, I was sure the pens were in the package. I opened it, and inside the box was a big stuffed bunny with a red wool sweater and a school-uniform plaid skirt. I dug in the box to see if the pens had somehow fallen under the bunny. No pens. Just the bunny.

Disappointed, I said dryly, "You got me a bunny. . . . Why?"

Glancing at Derek's facial expression, I could see I had said the wrong thing. He seemed to say, "You better clean this one up real quick." It was one of those moments of motherhood I'd really rather forget. I'm usually pretty good at hiding my feelings, and generally I don't have unrealistic expectations of the kids. I remember desperately wanting nothing more than to please my parents when I was a kid and the pain of falling short. Drawing on that memory, I pulled myself together and within seconds asked more excitedly this time, "So, why did you get me a bunny?"

"Because it made you smile," my daughter Janae said as the others nodded in full agreement.

171

Then they relayed how whenever I looked at the picture of the bunny, which happened several times because it was in one of our Christmas advertisements, they saw me smile. At one time, I had unconsciously commented on how cute it was and told them red was one of my favorite colors. Those were the hints they had picked up on. Never mind the big Christmas wish list on the refrigerator or the circled gel pens on sale in the office supply store advertisement. Those hints did not matter. They were motivated by my smile.

They wanted to get something to make me happy. They were right. Honestly, that stuffed bunny, whom I have since named Honey Bunny, is the best material gift I have ever received, because it still causes me to smile. As practical as gel pens would have been, they could not make me smile. Joy is something I don't often place as much of a priority on as I should. The kids knew that. Sometimes I just take myself too seriously, and I tire of always thinking deep thoughts. We all need to smile more. When we smile, we can enjoy mothering more, and our kids appreciate it too.

Let's face it, motherhood can be exhausting, especially once we have the revelation of our calling. This revelation causes us to press in all the more. We need God's grace. We need it to love our husbands so that our children will have a godly example of God's grace, love, and mercy. The Lord uses the marriage covenant to express a heavenly principle in an earthly realm. We need grace for those tough times when we don't exactly feel loving to our family or possess the wisdom of Solomon to referee whose turn it is to sit behind Mom in the car.

Grace and more grace is what we need. The apostle Paul called out for grace and found strength in his weakness. He learned to joy and boast in his weakness. God seems to enjoy manifesting himself in our weakness. So we moms need to lighten up. God wants us to have joy.

> **"A merry heart does good like medicine."**
> **Proverbs 17:22**

The Gift of Laughter

Proverbs 17:22 says, "A merry heart does good like medicine." Studies prove that when we laugh, vital endorphins are released in our bodies. These endorphins are not found in any medicine and can actually prolong life. Studies have proven that laughing, even watching our children and laughing at them, can prolong our lives. God sends us the gift of laughter in our children daily; after all, God laughs too.

In 2 Corinthians 12:9, God tells Paul his grace is sufficient for him. As a result, Paul makes a decision to boast in his weakness so that the power of Christ may rest upon him. In verse 10, Paul further makes a decision to take pleasure in infirmities, persecutions, distresses, and so on; for he realizes that when he is weak, God makes him strong. We know from this verse that God makes us strong in our weakness, and we also learn that we have to make the decision to take pleasure in that which may bother us the most. How can we take pleasure? We have to lighten up.

Our attitude affects everything. I have had mothers confess to me, often with great shame, "I just don't like my children." Be honest: haven't there been times when you said, "I love my children, but I do not like them"? This, by the way, is a misnomer, because in loving them we make the decision to like them too. We can learn to laugh at their childish irresponsibility, knowing that God laughs at our indiscretions. God gives mercy to us for our bad decisions. We owe a great debt to God, and we need to give grace to our children as well. We just need to lighten up.

Yes, our homes can be havens for the Holy Spirit, and we need to teach our children Scripture; but it all must be balanced in the context of joy. Paul took pleasure in his infirmities. He was not walking around with a "woe is me" attitude. We moms often quote 1 Thessalonians 5:17, which encourages us to pray without ceasing; however, do you realize that this Scripture is a sentence fragment? The sentence begins in verse 16, where we are told to rejoice always. Taking joy, having an attitude of joy, enables us to pray always. This is not a solemn holy act; it is a simple decision to be joyful. Children are just naturally funny. Even the most solemn children can make us laugh at times.

This is a challenge for me, as I tend to be introspective. My husband will come along and wrestle with the kids. He often has to say, "Lighten up, Cheryl." Generally, even when I do lighten up, it takes great effort. When everyone wants to go to the park for a quick bike ride, I think about the dirty dishes, the writing deadlines (often self-imposed), and the assignments I still need to check. I am learning to enjoy the moment and to be under the cloud of God's presence as he leads us to the promised land.

Enjoying the Moment

Moment by moment, God is teaching me that if I live in the future—what I have to do—I will forever be dissatisfied reaching for the elusive carrot that is not there. If I live in the past, I am weighed down by regrets that will constantly taunt. The only choice is to live in the present,

Ways to Recapture Our Joy

- Ride a bike.
- Swing.
- Do something you did as a child.
- Exercise.
- Make a craft—it stirs your creativity.
- Plan a let's-do-nothing day.
- Go on a scenic car ride.
- Paint a picture.

because I make the memories for tomorrow today. Those happy memories encourage me to press into tomorrow with promise.

Last night, we were invited out to dinner—quite unexpectedly. It was so much fun. It was a stretch for me to drop what I was doing to go, but I realized our children do not live in the strain of deadlines, under the heap of unfinished schoolwork or the weight of to-do lists. They live in the now, and they must experience joy in the moment. I want my children to continue to live a life of joy and to be able to pull from that reservoir as they get older and inevitably face hard times. Joyful attitudes don't just occur in the special times like birthdays and holiday celebrations, but in everyday life and pleasant surprises like a dinner invitation. These times are precious to our children.

One of my favorite plays is *Our Town*, by Thornton Wilder. In one of my favorite scenes, Becky, the main character, dies and gets an opportunity to revisit her ninth birthday, supposedly one of the happiest times of her life. The hectic preparations for a fun event like a birthday party overshadow the joy of the moment. Essentially, she is ignored. She realizes everyone is so consumed with preparations for the day that they have no time for her. They missed the real reason for the celebration. How often do we as moms do that?

We want the house perfect, the kids quiet, and everything in order. If everything is not in order, we shift into our must-do-it-now mode. Days with our children become consumed by activity, so much so that we miss the joy of the day. We see the dirty carpet instead of the tasty mud pies. Or we see the stained walls instead of the homemade Picasso. The to-dos of our day rob our joy. We have to reach deep within to find joy.

The joy of the Lord is our strength. As we choose joy, we find strength. We pray always, being joyful, knowing that God works all things out, not in our strength but in his. We can be joyful knowing that as we acknowledge and repent of our weaknesses, God delights in making us strong. Joy is a by-product of knowing God is going to work it all out even if we don't know how he will do it.

Our children are joyful because in a healthy family the weight of the world is not on them. They are free to experience joy. God has given them to us so that we too can be joyful. We experience genuine joy by looking through their eyes. I enjoy looking at Christmas lights, but when my children look at the neighborhood Christmas lights, my joy is taken to a new level. The oohs and aahs cause me to smile.

Children emit joy. In the book *Just David*, by Eleanor H. Porter, the main character, David, a boy who is separated from mainstream society by his father, is raised in the fullness of his childhood innocence. He thus learns to look at the world through pure eyes. Eventually a whole town is captured by his innocence and joy despite what happens to him. Joy is inherent in our children because for the most part there is no duplicity in them. We cannot take this from them, for the pure in heart see God. We should joy in raising our children every day with pure hearts.

So we have to lighten up when the laundry piles up, or we have to explain the distributive property for addition fifteen times, or the science experiment explodes all over our living room carpet. Ask the Lord to help you to laugh in the moment, to joy in the childhood of your children. Ask him to help you learn to laugh, even when the toilet has to be replaced because your child shoved a Lego block down it. Ask him to help you love them even when whose turn it is to set the dinner table becomes the battle of Bunker Hill. When we teach children to laugh at themselves, even sibling conflicts are reduced. Children learn the whole world does not rest on who sits behind Mommy in the van. Laughter diffuses tension.

I Need Your Grace

So we laugh and learn of God's grace. His grace is his strength to accomplish in us what we could not accomplish in ourselves. His grace enables us to get the laundry done, meditate on Scripture, and secure a godly heritage. Five minutes in God's grace will get more done than five years of our own efforts. We need to ask God for his grace. Daily we need his grace. God teaches us that his grace is sufficient in our weakness.

Grace also equips us to deal with the inner struggles of motherhood. This is especially true of moms who are still dealing with their own personal issues. Many moms struggle with feeling unworthy or have images of their children talking to a counselor about their withdrawal disorder due to forced toilet training. We may laugh, but most conscientious mothers have occasionally struggled with feelings of unworthiness. We compare ourselves to the supermom down the block who seems to homeschool her children, run the children's ministry, and go on a date with her husband three times a month. We wonder why we can't make it through the day without a sink of dirty dishes. It seems like other moms' children are smart, sensitive, and polite. They seem so well adjusted. We lose our joy when we compare ourselves to anyone.

Let's be honest: when we see someone doing better than us, we can have two reactions. We can deny that the family is really together. We rationalize that it's not what it seems to be. If we get past our cynicism and discover the family is genuine, our next response is to doubt ourselves or to project our ill-fated feelings onto our children. We become short-tempered or resort to some method to fix what we think is wrong. If we think our family should be more loving, we force them to embrace a method we heard our family pastor uses. Methods should motivate us to come to God, but they should never replace our relationship with God. In our insecurity, we often lean on methods.

For now, let's just deal with a mom's insecurity. It's natural and normal for all moms to doubt themselves. And while Christian moms should be immune to these feelings, we often feel them the most because we understand the awesome calling of motherhood. Usually, when we see misbehavior in our children, we look in the mirror. What did we do to cause it? How can we prevent it? We question ourselves. While this may be a good time for reflection, we cannot look too deeply, as proximity often distorts any image. Things seem like they are worse than they really are, and we want to work to fix them.

We work hard because we are so performance oriented. We think we must do things for God's approval. Thus, we think if we do the wrong thing, God won't act on our behalf. We get caught up, even consumed, with trying to do the right thing, expecting God to bless our actions. Sometimes he does. Often he won't, because that would reinforce a wrong mind-set. As we are striving and working hard, we miss the privilege of resting in his joy. Oh, how we need his grace.

His grace secures us. God likes to give us things we don't deserve, and he especially delights in giving them to those of us who feel we are undeserving. Instead of looking to resolve issues ourselves, we should look to the Lord; for in our weakness, he is strong. He's waiting for us to ask him, because he wants to help. There are only two conditions: we must ask him in faith (Heb. 11:6), and we must ask with sincere motives (James 4:3). This is where we moms often miss it. We are often unaware of our own motives.

Only God knows our hearts, and as he sheds his light on areas in our life, we must be quick to repent. Once we cry out to God, we must accept his grace and toss off the weight of our sin. God resists the proud but gives grace to the humble. Our weakness should draw us to God, for therein we find the strength to overcome. When we are weak, God makes us strong.

Searching for the Joy

As I mentioned earlier, when I first read the Scripture "Pray without ceasing" years ago, I thought it meant I had to be praying all day. Later I came to an understanding that I needn't talk all the time, but I need to be actively engaged in listening and responding. In other words, I thought I had to be serious and solemn all day just to hear God. I now know God joys in my pleasant disposition.

The context of that Scripture refers back to the encouragement to rejoice always (1 Thess. 5:16–17). Regularly being in a conversation with God about things and thoughts brings us joy. That is genuine communion with God—knowing he is personally and intimately involved with our daily lives. We simply need to listen for him with a joyful disposition.

Joy opens the door to blessing and helps us to hear God better.

Practically, the first thing we can do to relax and be joyful is cut down on some of our activities. This is easier said than done. We have to prayerfully consider what activities our kids will be involved in. Cut back on the times you are constantly running. While many understand this principle, some find it hard to implement because we fear our children may be left behind, or we have images of our child winning the world soccer cup and we dare not miss soccer for a season. Whatever your motives, surrender them to the Lord. Ask him to give you insight and wisdom to pare down your schedule so that you can schedule times for joyful activities.

I'm sure you've all heard it before: "Just say no." But I too have struggled with saying no and then felt guilty about it. I think as moms we are so conscientious that we want to help everyone. Everyone sees their request as important and as just one simple request.

Maintain some control of your time by having your own family goals. Having a goal or a vision makes it easy to say no to the distractions in your life. For instance, I love working with children but detest working out the mechanical details of anything. Therefore, if someone asks me to work on a project that involves technical aspects, I have no qualms saying no.

It's helpful to give a quick no but a slow yes. Generally, when someone asks me anything, I will say no but give the qualifier that I will think about it. That leaves the door open for me to say yes later if after I have prayed I really sense the need to help out. It's also easier to say no when I am rooted in my own goals.

People ask me to speak at functions or to write things for them quite frequently. I have to be more prayerful in this area. If I'm working on a project, it's easy to say no. I have also learned to sincerely pray that others will find the help they need when I have to say no. I seek God's grace to hide me in my weakness. Sometimes people have told me after they finished a project, "Oh, Cheryl, I did not even think of you." Oh, God's grace! He protected me from even trying to stretch myself too thin. What joy!

Besides relaxing our schedules, we must learn to relax our minds. We moms do pride ourselves on thinking and doing ten different things at a time. This is not necessarily a beneficial discipline when it comes to God's grace, because we keep trying to do things in our strength. We cannot ask God to reveal his will and maintain our control of the situation. We have to let go and know joyfully that God's grace is working.

Prayer Brings Joy

Prayer also brings joy to our lives. Jesus tells us to ask, that our joy may be full (John 16:24). There is joy in being able to ask Jesus anything. Being joyful is easier for me if people are praying for me or if I am practicing purposeful thinking. I used to hear people say, "I could feel the prayers"; but I truly never experienced it. Recently, I was going through some hard times and needed people to pray for me. I asked, and I could actually feel the prayers getting me through the situation. Now I ask people to pray for me regularly.

Mother prayer groups and small intercessory groups are best. I have a small circle of friends I pray with and for. Mother prayer groups need to be rooted in godly leadership that has integrity. I have seen groups where the leader used the prayer as a guise to advance her own agenda or to hide from the sin in her life by praying for others. Ouch! Yes, before we can pray for others, we must humbly approach

More Ways to Recapture Our Joy

- Plan a family vacation with no schedule or no sightseeing.
- Make your favorite childhood recipe.
- Play a game with your kids.
- Do something you've never done before.
- Color in a coloring book.

the throne for ourselves. I am talking not about perfection but about an attitude of repentance. Repentance, as we discussed in chapter 6, is a lifestyle and openness to God where we admit our wrong, accept correction, and turn around and not return to our sin. The Scriptures are our guideline. First Timothy 3 states that deacons or godly leaders should have their homes in order. Look for godly traits of repentance and openness to God in all your leaders. Mothers of Preschoolers (MOPS) and Home by Choice (see the list in the appendix) are viable options if there is no mothers' group in your local church.

Generally, we have peace, joy, and quietness of soul when we are in God's divine purpose. Pray to remove all distractions, and purpose to do all you do for the glory of God, knowing that he finds glory in your mopping floors, washing dirty dishes, and ministering to your family. The most obvious way to succeed is to engage your children in this process with you.

Fun in the Spiritual Disciplines

The spiritual disciplines can be fun. Add some practical activities, like discussing Scripture with others, and watch your Bible reading time come alive. Challenge your children to do the same. Our children all have Bible translations they can understand, and we graduate them as they get older.

You may start toddlers out with picture Bibles. Discuss what's in the picture. Relate toddler Bible reading (or picture reading) to family reading so your toddler can join in the conversation. Do the same with easy-reading Bibles. Older children can discuss with the adults. We really like the New International Reader's Version of the Bible for our in-between readers. Our children seem to enjoy advancing through the different translations of the Bible.

We schedule a quiet time in our home when the kids can read or pray quietly or journal what the Lord may be saying to their hearts. Scheduling this time is often challenging. We are working to establish this time daily, but we implement it immediately when we see as a family we need it. We look for fun Bible questions and try to challenge one another to find the answer in our daily Bible reading.

Prayer can be fun. We make family prayer stations. In our living room or another large space, we position in a circle items that represent different people or things to pray for. Since little ones like to move around and touch tangible things, this is a great tool for all ages. I have used world- or state-map puzzles to pray for governments, countries, and states; index cards with specific prayer requests; photographs of people we are praying for; kitchen utensils to pray for world hunger; empty medicine bottles to pray for the sick; and newspaper clippings to pray for news events and government officials.

Movement gives children a tangible understanding of what they are praying for. And if it's perceived as a game, that's okay, at first. It is the consistency and sensitivity of prayer that you are building. Children also begin to associate prayer with fun, or joy; therefore, quiet time for them will not be drudgery, as they will be able to relate it back to having fun.

Likewise, encourage your children to pray for one another. Yes, they should pray for the world, but they will see

Movement gives children a tangible understanding of what they are praying for.

immediate response to their prayers for siblings and family. Prayer builds intimacy and reduces sibling rivalry. Many of my spiritual breakthroughs have been the result of my children praying for me.

We have used a family prayer box to make prayer joyful for our children. Our family prayer box is an old baby-wipes box. We put requests in it from people who ask us to pray for them. We date the prayers and pray over the box intermittently. Sometimes we set it in the middle of the dinner table so that we will remember to pray.

We have also made prayer wheels. I learned this concept from Ed and Glenda Corley of Berean Ministries. They talked about praying within your sphere of influence, and I adapted the idea to use with our children. In the core of my circle are the kids and Derek. In the first outer circle are church, extended family, and covenant friends. In the next circle is government—community, county, state, and federal. In the final circle are people of the world. The circles are on heavy cardboard, and the kids can pass them around freely. This gives them something visual and tangible. The circles have a diameter of about twelve inches. Each prayer concern is inscribed on one circle, although you can make smaller circles if you like. When my children were very young, we used to march around the circles as we prayed.

Take drawing paper, place it on the floor, and draw outlines of the inner and outer courts. If you are very creative, you can make your own tabernacle out of boxes or wood. It does not have to be perfect. I actually give the children prayer requests and ask them to pray for the individual or situation as they enter the tabernacle.

I use the tabernacle to drive home the point that they have to be single-minded when they are praying. As the

Still More Ways to Recapture Our Joy

- Read a Dr. Seuss book to your kids.
- Play an old song from your childhood.
- Make a paper airplane and throw it at your husband or the kids.
- Dance to a funny song with your kids.
- Plan a let's-do-everything-backward day.

kids step into each drawn component of the tabernacle, I encourage them to just think about what they are praying about. They are not allowed to turn and talk to siblings or even me. They must talk only to God. I tell them as they enter the tabernacle that they are approaching God's throne. The kids like closing their eyes because it helps them concentrate.

This exercise is not for toddlers or preschoolers but is more appropriate for older elementary children whom you want to teach to become more focused or fervent in prayer and less distracted. It is also a good exercise for adults who tend to let their minds wander during prayer. "The effectual fervent prayer of a righteous man availeth much" (James 5:16 KJV), and this exercise teaches children to be focused and passionate in a natural way.

Role-playing stories is a way to joyfully study the Bible as a family. One of the best role-plays we did was when the kids pretended to be Jesus's disciples in the boat and each child had a turn being Peter. Mom and Dad were Jesus, bidding them to come. I gained insight as the other kids in the boat yelled distracting things to Peter, such as, "You're going to sink!" "Wait, Peter, that's not really Jesus," "It's a ghost," or "Be careful." These kinds of statements were constantly assailed at the mock Peter until, often in frustration, the child would turn around to hush his or her boat comrades. Interestingly, the scenario was repeated each time with new distracting comments. We have also role-played young Samuel and likewise received great insight into being awakened by the voice of God.

Role-playing is a great way to motivate private Bible study, as each person has to read the Bible story alone before we come together as a family. Of course, when the children were younger, we read the Bible story to them. This is a fond family memory.

You can illustrate biblical concepts concretely. For instance, the importance of choosing our words before we say them can be illustrated by giving each child a jar of sand. We usually just get ours from a beach visit. We pour out the sand and ask the child to pick up each grain because we didn't mean to pour it all out. Frustrated, the child will come to the conclusion that he or she cannot pick up the all the sand. This realization can later be reinforced because of the emotional and tangible connection made with the experience. When you correct your children later when they use their words rashly, they will easily be able to recall the sand and how they felt as they tried to put it back into the jar. Children learn better by example than by lecture.

We also have biblical confessions that our children recite regularly, along with hand motions to help remember them. We have attached Scripture to their names. Here is what my children say:

My name is Jarrett Gregory Carter. I am Defender of the Truth. Jesus Christ is truth. I daily live this truth.

My name is Janae Joy Carter. I am God's Gracious Gift of Joy. In God's presence is fullness of joy, and I daily live in God's presence.

186

My name is Jolene Talitha Carter. I am increasing in God's glory and anointing every day. I am a young lady of impeccable character, grace, and charm.

(All three children recite) Great is my peace because my parents delight themselves in you, Lord. Every day, including today, I increase in wisdom, stature, and favor with God and humankind. Wealth and riches are in my hand. Wisdom is my best friend. No weapon formed against me shall prosper.

You may use a simple Scripture that your children can memorize. If your child has a name with a negative meaning, turn it to the positive. For instance, if a child's name means "bitterness," simply say, "I am bitter against anything that is not like God." Jabez, of the now-famed *The Prayer of Jabez*, understood this principle. His name means "bitter," but he turned what could have been a negative around by praying that he would cause no harm and that God's hand would be with him. Centuries later, Jabez's prayer would inspire a nation.

Make a family altar or quiet room. We used to have a quiet room, and I suggest that if you have space, you have one in your home. It will also help you to approach prayer with joy and consistency. Decorate it to be inviting. You may even put two chairs in it, with one representing your invitation for Jesus to come in and have a seat. For us it was a great place for biblical meditation.

When you really need your joy and the grace of God to be upon you, go into your bedroom or bathroom or wherever you can get to quickly, close the door, and call out to God to fill you afresh. Tell your children that unless they see blood, you don't want to be disturbed. My children have come to appreciate my going a few times behind a closed door, especially if it seems like I'm going to lose it.

> **Make a decision to daily choose joy. Give God a joyful attitude and watch what he gives you in return.**

Susanna Wesley, the mother of John and Charles Wesley, was known to throw her apron over her head and pray in the middle of the day. She had a brood of nineteen, although only ten lived to adulthood. She had the discipline of quieting herself internally. I suspect this method got the children to leave her alone. This works best if you start them young.

Sometimes if I burst spontaneously into prayer, my children will join in. God is not a creepy thing to them, but he's fun. Of course, I'm no Susanna Wesley, but I do need intermittent times of prayer in the midst of my day to keep me joyful. I once read, "We need to pray often, pray much, and pray intensely to move the hand of God." I believe that. Trust God with your inabilities and insecurities, and he will fill you with his grace. Even those who feel they have it together need God's grace and mercy. Let's purpose to be joyful as we daily submit to him.

Why Is Joy So Important?

Our attitude of joy affects our relationship with the Lord. We know we can trust God, but can God trust us? Every night I administer flaxseed oil to the children as a healthy supplement to their diets. At first, they used to scrunch their faces and give me a hard time each time I gave them a dose. Lately they have really complied with me, and I appreciate their cooperation. It makes the whole experience pleasant for all of us. The Lord spoke to my heart and said, "That's why I appreciate a joyful attitude. It makes it pleasant for me."

We always think of what God can do for us. A joyful attitude is something we can give God. Make a decision to daily choose joy. Give God a joyful attitude and watch what he gives you in return.

Prayer

Lord, today I give you a joyful attitude. Take it and use it for your glory.

10

Do You Hear Him?

Hearing God in Our Hearts and in Our Homes

A little girl once wrote to God, "When you are silent, I wonder if you're there. God, when you are silent, I wonder if you care." This little girl thought her prayers were on their way to heaven but kept getting stuck in the clouds. That little girl was me. Occasionally I still feel like that. When God is silent, do you ever wonder if he cares?

Perhaps I'm being too analytical, but it has always bothered me that the children of Israel were in bondage four hundred years. If you think about their bondage not as a historical fact but as people's day-to-day existence, it might bother you a little bit too. Generations of people, God's chosen people, lived in utter despair with a vague hope that somehow their children's lives would be different. When you think about this, you might be able to understand their initial reaction to Moses when he arrived as God's deliverer. They did not believe that God really cared about them. Exodus 6:9 says they did not listen to Moses because of their discouragement and cruel bondage.

Give ear and come to me; hear me, that your soul may live.

Isaiah 55:3

All of us relish the triumphant parting of the Red Sea, but can we understand the Israelites' pain and hopelessness that passed effortlessly from one generation to the other like a useless heirloom? We cannot fathom their despair any more than we can that of enslaved Africans in America. The Scripture "And God heard their groaning" (Exod. 2:24 KJV) has always bothered me. Come on, doesn't it bother you that he did not hear them even after the first one hundred years of captivity? Why did it take four hundred years for him to respond?

I also struggle with what historians call the four hundred years of silence between Malachi and Matthew. I know God was not really silent, but we have no record of his dealings with his people. These things unsettle me in light of Lazarus being raised from the dead or any of the other mass of miracles God performed in both the Old and New Testaments. It seems he can perform a miracle anytime he wants to, and I wonder why at times he chooses to do nothing—or so it seems to me. I know God is not silent, and I know his plan for me is perfect. I know that he loves me. I know he is not holding back on me. All these things I know, but his seeming silence still troubles me, even today.

I wonder if the children of Israel ever got to the point where they simply yearned for God. Did they ever get the revelation that they were God's chosen people and they didn't have to live as slaves? At what point did they cry out with their whole hearts to God? I guess I will never know on this side of eternity. All I do know is that God is very much involved in our lives and speaking to us all the time. He yearns to communicate with us more than we

191

can ever know. It is just a matter of acknowledging our need for him.

The bottom line is that we need God. We desperately need to hear his voice, and when we're desperate, we'll do just about anything. Isn't that why we chase after him? Although we know he's not running away, it's as we hunger and thirst for him and seek his face that ultimately the door opens to hear his voice.

There are a few practical things we can do. We have already discussed making your home amenable to the Spirit of God and having a joyful and expectant attitude. With all those preliminaries out of the way, let's get down to the nitty-gritty of hearing God's voice.

When it comes to hearing God, often we think about our struggle to hear what God is saying in an external sense. We believe that somehow the messages must get from heaven to us. The truth is that Christ lives in our heart, and it is our heart that sometimes impedes our ability to hear him. Our heart hinders our hearing by hiding its true self from us. None of us knows our true self. We might think we do, but only God sees clearly; for he says, "My thoughts are not your thoughts, neither are your ways my ways" (Isa. 55:8).

Christianity That Transforms

Christianity has become marginalized to a code of moral behavior, but it is so much more than that. It is being transformed through a vibrant, living relationship with our Savior. It takes work. It takes time. Being a Christian is more than adhering to a code of conduct. I used to admire people who, as I saw it, got the privilege to be with other Christians all day. Surely, I thought, they must float in the office and greet one another with a holy kiss and have prayer meetings around the watercooler. I am assured by many who work with other Christians, as well as by personal experience, that this is generally not the case. But why?

There are many reasons, but largely I think it has to do with the transformation process. While we are all striving to be like Christ and die to ourselves, we are each at different levels of crucifixion. One of us is compelled to love his brother and has the revelation to press beyond the proverbial comfort zone. Yet this same individual is so mission-minded he has no time for private devotions. Still another of us understands that the church must rise to a level of excellence, and this passion drives her to succeed against all odds. Unfortunately, that same passion compels her to be intolerant of others' shortcomings. Get it? We must constantly be on guard lest the enemy pervert the good in us to evil.

Balancing Everything

As moms, our selfless service to our families can get out of balance as we use it to substitute for our relationship with God. This impedes our hearing. God may direct you to skip a family vacation and take a family missionary trip to Uganda instead. Are you going to cast that thought away or ask God for clarity? We must not allow our devotion to our family to keep us from God. Now please keep balance here. God will not tell you to leave, ignore, or neglect your children or husband to do anything for him. This would violate his character. I am simply saying we cannot idolize our family.

Idolizing our family also keeps us in denial. Many times I have spoken with families in crisis, I mean real crisis—wayward children, drug abuse, and so on—and had moms come to me crying that their children used to be good God-fearing children. However, most times these parents were in denial about character flaws that became full-blown sin lifestyles in their children.

Recognizing and dealing with the sin in our children isn't easy. It's easy to deny it and, therefore, do nothing about it. A predominant attitude I see in moms is to expect the world to bend to Johnny. His teachers and the youth pastor must understand Johnny, instead of bringing him to a point of repentance. All of our children need correction. As parents, we should find our identity not in them but in the finished work of Christ Jesus, because when we define ourselves through them, we miss the mark with God.

I wish I could say that I've never been guilty of missing the mark. I have erred more times than I care to count. I say this not with solemn resignation but with profound grief. Am I a bad person? No, I am probably a lot like you. Sometimes I do the right thing, and other times I do the wrong thing.

I'm so proud of myself when I hold my tongue, resist jealousy, ignore pettiness, and press into kingdom thinking when it would be so much easier to lean on my own understanding. Likewise, I am grieved when I take the low ground. It's not that I desire total perfection of myself all the time, but I do expect a high degree of moral excellence, based on my calling and, more importantly, my relationship with Christ. I remain committed to a strong sense of Christian duty, immersed in moving beyond mere profession and into genuine lifestyle transformation. Aren't all Christians?

Being a Christian is more than a confession at the altar. It's more than attending church. It's more than just loving our brother. It's more than praying day and night. It is daily getting on the altar and staying there until our lives become a sacrifice to the Lord. Many of the saints of old possessed this quality. They understood death to self marks the transformation process. It is not talked about much in the church today. We are so busy making our plans, working our plans, and asking God to bless our plans that we have forgotten the Master Planner. Our plans are often not God's plans.

Hearing His Voice Every Day

We can only know God's plans to the degree we hear his voice. Hearing God is vital to the Christian life. What does God's voice sound like? In Genesis 3:8, Adam and Eve heard the voice of the Lord God walking in the garden. I've wondered: why did they hear his voice as he walked, and where was God when they were sinning? The children of Israel heard the thunder and lightning. Jonah heard God's voice under a juniper tree as he sat and felt sorry for himself after the people of Nineveh repented. I guess the sound of God's voice depends on where you're at and what you're thinking when you hear him. We may not all agree on the sound of his voice, but we can certainly agree on the results.

God speaks in a way to get our attention. He spoke in a burning bush that was not consumed. He knew something about that sight would draw Moses to it. Anyone else upon seeing it might have run away. The Lord deals with each of us in such a personal way. He uses anything he can get his hands on. He'll use a donkey if he has to. We need not look for a divine supernatural happening, because God is in our hearts, and he primarily speaks to us in our hearts. We have to turn our heads in his direction and incline our ear.

God speaks to us every day, in our daily choices, in our conversations with our children, and in our interactions with others. It isn't hard to hear God in the everyday. It is hard for us to stop and make the adjustment. In our

God speaks in a way to get our attention.

noisy world, it's easy to ignore his gentle prodding.

Recently, I went to the mall and noticed an educational store was going out of business. The kids and I went inside, as we had planned to do anyway, when we noticed a sign that read, "40–60 percent off everything in the store." Gently it occurred to me that many of the prices may have been raised to reflect the seemingly high discount. Derek and I had been discussing budget issues, and that information helped me to really look at the items that were genuinely discounted. God was speaking to me because he understood our family finances. Some may consider that a little thing, but God is not just there in big spectacular megameetings but in the meaningful small moments.

Now here's the scary part. I acknowledged the initial prodding, but as the kids and I started excitedly tossing items in the shopping cart, the thought seemed more distant. When I got to the register, again it occurred to me that the discounts had not been taken on some items, that indeed the prices had been inflated; but at that point, in my head, I had already bought the items, if you know what I mean. We were already at home playing with that Grown-ups vs. Kids game, and I was serving popcorn as we played. My own desires prevented me from heeding God's voice even while standing at the cash register when I had the opportunity to repent and put the overpriced items back.

Our desires can actually keep us from hearing God. Remember the story from chapter 5 about how my daughter used to climb on the counter and get a cookie? Once she retrieved a cookie, she would come to me and ask if she could have the cookie. She was holding it and smelling it, and the only thing left to do was taste it. We are like that with God many times. We are holding on to our desires, and we cannot hear God telling us no, because we want what we want when we want it. Our desire to have what we want outweighs our desire to hear God.

It's a heart issue. Our desires must be God's desires. We moms must want to do his will, even as much as we want the other things. James and John's mom came and asked Jesus for her sons to be on each side of Jesus. Do you realize she was asking for them to be crucified with Jesus? Our thoughts are so small. So as mothers, we must continually give them over to God and ask him about his desires for us, our husbands, and our children.

Hearing Him Clearly

If you're having difficulty hearing God, ask him for a pure heart and deal with the blatant sin in your life. This is not to condemn you; it is a loving conviction that urges you to grow up in him and promises you a reward as a result of that growth. God rewards those who diligently seek him. Do you know what the reward of seeking God is? More of God! When you seek him earnestly, he gives you more of himself.

Press in if you want more of God. Sometimes pressing in requires we come up higher in our thinking. Once after I spoke at a luncheon, I jokingly asked Derek, "Did I offend anyone?"

He playfully teased, "No more than usual."

But I knew I had. I had spoken beyond what was necessary to be said and used illustrations that were too personal just to get the audience to agree with me. I knew why I had done it too. I feared the people. As I looked at their faces, more than anything else I wanted their approval. I began to expound on things I needn't have developed and sought approval by trying to get the audience on my side. In short, I had sinned with my tongue.

Journaling

Journaling is an important spiritual discipline. We know about the victorious feats and struggles of saints from the early church because they kept journals. Actually, the epistles are merely letters, a kind of journaling too. Recording our spiritual journey is an important part of spiritual growth. It helps us to see and hear God in our daily activities.

There is no specific way to keep a journal. The key is to be as consistent as possible. I like to get a pretty floral design, as that motivates me to write. Of course, you can use just a regular notebook.

I felt God speaking to me about my tongue, and at first I resolved never to speak anywhere publicly again, but even I knew this was not possible. God wants us to operate in temperance or moderation in all we do. It would have been easier for me not to speak than to develop temperance in my expressions. Temperance is not keeping silent but knowing when to speak. It is a vital skill in Christian growth. You see, for years the Lord had dealt with me about an unbridled tongue, and now he was dealing with me about speaking in moderation. That's much harder for me than just to keep quiet. I'd rather not say anything than say just enough so that a word is "fitly spoken."

This wasn't the first time I had been corrected by the Lord. He has challenged me and changed me in so many ways over the years. It is in these quiet moments with the Lord where I have grown the most. I have heard great sermons, been inspired by awesome praise and worship music, and attended some powerful prayer meetings, and collectively all these have spurred my spiritual growth. But by far the most transforming moments of my life have occurred when God spoke to me personally.

Hasn't it been the same for you? It's not when you're sitting in church on Sunday morning that matters most, but how much of the church sits in you on Thursday afternoon, or when your child keeps whining about applesauce after you've told her ten times there is no more in the house. The rubber meets the road when we can daily give ourselves completely over to God so he can change us. God does do things corporately at times, but I've found he delights in doing things in a quiet, personal way in our dialogue with him.

When I morally erred in speaking too rashly at the luncheon, God spoke to me and corrected me, and it didn't matter who was around me; I had heard God and repented. That was a quiet time between me and God. It was not in a prescribed time frame, but God spoke and I heeded. In the formative years of motherhood, young moms might do well to cast off the guilt and allow God to speak to their hearts wherever and whenever he wants to. This is not a radical statement, but most of us have been acculturated to believe God only speaks in our scheduled quiet time.

God communicates with us all the time. The keen ear leans in his direction. In my case, I knew the Lord was calling me to move into a level of temperance or moderation. Notice, anything the Lord says to you can be directly traced back to Scripture, because the Spirit and the Word agree. God will never speak something that contradicts his Word or his character. Thus we can hear the voice of God better by understanding the character of God better.

Getting to Know God Better

God is patient, kind, and long-suffering. These qualities define God himself. God does not just love. He is love. Love personified is God. In the same way, Jesus does not just tell the truth. He is truth. The essence of his being is truth. Those who come face-to-face with Jesus behold the truth. These are infinite ideas to wrap our finite minds around.

199

Yet if we don't stretch to understand God beyond our human constraints, we will forever be searching for answers. Too often man has brought God down to an understanding on his terms. Thus we have made God in our own image. This should not be. We are made in God's image. So we must determine to come up higher, to go up to Zion, the place of worship, to hear the voice of God. This requires getting rid of the sin in our lives. Our hearts must be cleansed.

Besides being cleansed, our hearts must likewise be circumcised. The good must be cut away to make room for the best. Cutting out the good to get to the best is really hard because it may be painful. For instance, the Lord may require we give up being a Sunday school teacher so we can devote that time to teaching our own children; or he may require we stop talking to our friends about our problems and talk to him instead. This is a very personal issue. You have to be willing to ask God to circumcise your heart after cleansing your heart.

Stay committed to God. Walk in immediate forgiveness, forsake sin, and continue to press in to know God more. Every day we should be more like Jesus. We can likewise ask our children and husbands to join us in this journey. Even as Moses had to take off his shoes as he approached the presence of God, so too we must come in holiness and humbleness. Our hearts must be singularly his so we can hear him clearly.

As you first start your journey to get to know God better, reach out to him. He has promised to reach out to you. Besides looking for God and inviting him in to change your heart, there are a few other practical things you can do to hear God better. Review your day with God. Journaling is an excellent activity that really helps you to hear God as you review your day and focus on the things God has done in your life. There are many different kinds of journals.

Kinds of Journals

- Gratitude journal—Take time at the end of the day to review your day and thank God for the many blessings he's given you that day. This type of journal helps us to see the hand of God in our day-to-day activities.
- Prayer journal—Writing our prayers out during quiet time helps to focus our prayers. It also gets us a personal historic record of our prayers.
- Letter journal—Write a letter to another about something you have learned or a move of God in your life. I like writing letters to my children to give to them when they are older.
- Parent journal—You may journal about your child's physical, emotional, and spiritual development. Cite specific things you would like to remember and how God works with you through each stage of development.
- Question-and-answer journal—Ask God a question and wait on him to reveal the answer to you. This type of journaling requires a grave level of spiritual maturity so that you don't write your own thoughts. Also, your answers may not come for a long period of time. You have to be comfortable with this time lag. This isn't used as a fortune-telling, predict-the-future type journal but more of a character-building exercise.

Gratitude journals, which record the process of you personally thanking God daily, help you to see the hand of God on an intimate level. This kind of journaling is best done before bed when you can review the details of your day.

If we want to hear God, we have to be ready to listen to him. Therefore, we should invite him into our day-to-day activities. Ask him to help you be more patient or more consistent with your children. You will notice that the more you acknowledge God, the more you will see him. It really is simple. He has been there all along, but when we take the time to seek him, we always find him.

Pray that you hear God's voice clearly. Take authority over the enemy using Scripture (Luke 10:17–19). Do not fear the enemy. Ask God to confirm his Word to you. You may do this by asking him to confirm it in your Bible study, by meditation, or through channels that are uniquely his choosing. Now I'm not talking spooky stuff here, just a real heart-to-heart with God where he confirms his Word in a clear way.

Remember, God will never contradict his Word. Also remember to apply his Word in context. Godly counselors provide a safe haven from the weird stuff. Proverbs 11:14 says, "In the multitude of counsellors there is safety" (KJV), so never do anything on your own without checking out what you think you've heard. I depend on my husband and mature friends to help sort things out at times. No matter where you are in your spiritual growth, accountability is essential.

Another practical way to hear the voice of God is to write down things that are impressed upon your mind. Generally, your quiet or meditation time is best to record your thoughts, but you may get a special journal. Some find it helpful to ask God a question and to genuinely wait for his response. I have found this method stretches me, especially because I am often tempted just to write down my own thoughts. I have to really force myself to wait on God. I think he delights in molding me in this area too.

Questions are a great way to press into God. When I ask a question and he doesn't answer me right away, it motivates me to move beyond my specified prayer time. I search for him in my daily routine. This expectancy has been nurtured over the years with answered prayer. Sometimes God has cleansed my heart so I could see an obvious answer; other times he has stretched me to come up higher in my thinking, like when he talked to me about speaking in moderation. Also remember, if you want profound answers, ask stimulating questions.

While we are growing in hearing God's voice, I am reminded of George Mueller. He used to pray in such a way that he got to a point that whether God said yes or no, it did not matter, because his heart was not inclined in either direction. This is really hard for many of us. With our words we state we are asking God, but our hearts are crying out in a particular direction. Most of us have desires, sometimes even hidden from ourselves, such that we do not see the wretchedness in our own hearts. Therefore, when we ask God for something, we are most apt to mishear him in an area where we have strong emotional attachments. Be careful when praying for your child or husband that you are sincerely praying God's will and not your own.

I highly recommend *How to Hear the Voice of God in a Noisy World* by Teresa Seputis. Her ideas are very practical and easy for moms to implement in their everyday lives. She makes the point that each of us has a predominant way in which God speaks to us. Does he show you pictures? Does he mainly speak to you in the Scriptures? Usually, whatever pattern he speaks to you in is your dominant way of hearing. You can learn to comfortably rely on this area to hear accurately.

Moms, we just need to be confident that God is speaking to us and that he is right there with us all day. Talk to him throughout the day. When you first begin this practice, it may seem strange, but as you see and hear him, it will become more natural. Ask him to cleanse your heart and to circumcise the activities of your day. I must caution that as we grow to hear God's voice, we must never step out of the biblical realm. God will never violate his own Word, the Bible. He will never cause you to do anything illegal, immoral, unethical, or unholy. I've heard people say crazy things like, "God told me to leave my husband." This is absolutely ridiculous.

Inherent in hearing God better is the danger that we will attempt to use him for personal gain. That's why hearing God is first and foremost a heart issue. We must remain humble, holy, and happy to be used for God's pleasure. We are his instruments; he is not ours. Therefore, we must diligently search our hearts as to why we want God more. When you find you are always in the "gimme" mode or no longer enjoy the presence of God, you are probably on the slippery slope of self-centeredness and sin.

Our walk with God is authenticated by our crucifixion of the flesh. As we spend time with God, we should become more and more like him. Once we hear God's voice, we must be willing to be obedient, for therein lies our true love for the Lord. If we genuinely obey him, we are his. We are his sheep, and we do hear his voice. By faith we must believe this and meditate on it. The most valuable entity to God is a pure heart and a faith-filled life. Moms, this is not always easy. We lay ourselves on the altar daily and stretch our arms toward heaven, knowing God fills a broken, yet yielded, vessel.

There is a danger also in thinking God is speaking new things to us all the time. Often he just wants us to walk faithfully in the old thing, much like we remind our children to do something until they get it right. God does the same thing with us. He prods us along. We can avoid deception when we know God is not going to give us a grand new thing to do if we haven't been successful with the old.

What Did You Say, Lord?

God is a holy God. The patriarchs of the Bible understood this and trembled when he spoke. The deity of God can be easily dismissed in our making God so common. We must balance God's love for humanity with his awesome being.

He is the great I Am, the Creator of heaven and earth. To be in relationship with a holy God costs something. I once heard someone say, "Salvation is free, but it is not cheap." There is a level of holiness that is required to hear the voice of God. Our hearts must be his.

> **There is a level of holiness that is required to hear the voice of God. Our hearts must be his.**

Peter Lord, in his book *Hearing God*, talks about cleansing and circumcising our hearts. This is key. Our hearts must be cleansed from sin. It is not enough to say, "I am sorry." We must live a life of repentance that cries out to God. Purity of heart is the issue. The Bible says the pure in heart will see God. Those with pure hearts are those who get to the root of issues.

Scripture informs us that David had a heart after God's own heart. He was a repentant man. Sometimes repentance takes time. Bible scholars say David's repentance may have taken a year or more from the time he had an affair with Bathsheba and had Uriah killed. Yet when David came face-to-face with his sin, he repented. The issue was that when David saw himself, he genuinely repented. He never went back to his former sin.

We too must have holy hearts. When God points out our sin, we must be quick to repent and to deal with the cause of the sin in our lives. For instance, one time I had lied about something. I went to the Lord clutching 1 John 1:9 firmly under my arm. He did forgive me, but he also talked to me about the root of the sin and why I felt the need to lie. It was then he began to teach me the biblical concept of "serving many out of serving One." He is the One I serve, and through serving him, I am freed from the tyranny of trying to be all things to all people.

God wants to get to the root of the sin in our lives. He wants us fully transformed. In Jesus's illustrative teaching on the vine in John 15, we learn some essential truths. First, and most importantly, we learn we must abide in the vine, who is Jesus. He is our anchor, and he declares his Father is the vinedresser.

Next we learn that once we abide in him, if we produce little fruit, we will be pruned. Pruning is an often uncomfortable, sometimes painful process. He must take those things out of our lives that hinder our growth. It may be a bad attitude, an idle use of our time, or gossip under the guise of prayer. These things hinder us from receiving all that God has for us. He cleanses us from these so that we will be holy and hear him better. Sin blocks our reception. We need pure hearts to hear God. We must joy in this process, because it will yield the peaceable fruit of righteousness.

It is our willingness and graciousness to let God do in our lives what must be done that will hasten the process. If God speaks to us, we must say, as David did, "Yes, Lord, you are justified in your justice" (see Ps. 51:4). He was saying, "God, you are right." He did not buck against the hand of God. He cooperated with the process.

We also learn that another kind of branch is pruned. This is for the mature Christian. The Lord will remove the good in our lives to make way for the best. In this case, what's removed is not the sin in your life but things that weight you down and keep you from pressing into the presence of God. This kind of pruning is often misunderstood, as sometimes we may think God is only concerned about the sin in our lives. But he wants us to live in a level of holiness.

We are made in God's image. Sin is not our true nature; holiness is. When we arrive at this point in God, he strips us of our perceived good to make way for the best. He circumcises our hearts, cutting away the excess in our lives. As this weight drops off, we will be able to hear him clearly.

Some may wonder what is going on when they don't hear God. There are several possible things going on. First, perhaps you are not tuned to him. Often we expect God to speak in the spectacular, not in the ordinary. Look for him in the ordinary, in the regular rhythm of your day.

We are made in God's image. Sin is not our true nature; holiness is.

Second, confess all known sin. You may also ask the Lord to search your heart and reveal sin to you. He wants to be in fellowship with you just as much as you want to be in communion with him. You may also want to go back to the last thing he told you to do and see if you have done it. Ask him where you have erred.

Finally, sometimes in the circumcision process, he is calling you to come up higher. Once I said to the Lord, "Why don't you just explain something to me in an easier way?"

He impressed to me, "I want you to come up higher." Keep pressing into God. As long as there is breath in our bodies, we can make a decision for God.

Hearing God is imperative as we learn to press into God. God wants to talk with us. He is willing. He is waiting. As we call out to him, we must expect him to hear. By faith, we believe he wants a deep, intimate relationship with us. Today he speaks to you. He whispers in your ear, "Want to know my secrets?" He reveals his secrets to his friends. He does not delight in being mysterious. He wants friendship and companionship. He stands with arms outstretched to those who have wandered away from him. He longs for you. He looks for you. Come, and hear what he has to say to you.

Prayer

Lord, I make a decision to hear you every day. I will look for you, and I will find you.

11

The Finish Line

Standing Strong Spirit, Soul, and Body

I squirmed in my seat as I noticed the text for the Mother's Day message—Proverbs 31. There it was again—gnawing at me. Taunting me, telling me I should be making clothes for my family, cooking gourmet meals, running my own home business, balancing the checkbook; in short, being supermom, superwife, and super-Christian. For a moment, just a microsecond, I was tempted to fall into self-pity again, but suddenly the realization hit me. Scripture does not command me to be like the Proverbs 31 woman. I am commanded to be like Jesus.

As I thought about it, I realized I was more like Jesus than I was the day before. By his grace I was becoming more patient, kind, and long-suffering. I was discovering his unique plan for my life, and as a result I was being fashioned into the woman he wanted me to be. Once I released myself and listened to the message, the speaker affirmed my thoughts. She explained that Proverbs 31 represents a privileged woman in her senior season of life. She had servants and many advantages. Clearly, her children were old enough to call her blessed. What a revelation that was to me!

This freed me. I also realized that it's very important for us moms to nurture ourselves. We do a great job of beating up on ourselves, and we're great at caring for others but lousy at tending to our own needs. We have to nurture ourselves and get filled up so we can serve others. Most importantly, we need to be filled with the zeal of the Lord. We must be equipped to make it to the spiritual finish line with him. We must care for ourselves—spirit, soul, and body. Humbly and tenderly we have to learn to submit our lives every day to the Lord, knowing he alone cares for us.

Taking Care of Your Body

The body is important because it is the vehicle by which we serve God and our families. We should eat right and get adequate rest and sleep. Incidentally, these two are not synonymous. I have found I need to get sleep, but during the day I need to plan regular times of rest when I sit or lie down. Your first response is probably, "That's impossible"; but if you prayerfully look at your schedule and pare it a bit, you may find time. This is especially true for mothers with endless-energy toddlers. You cannot pray effectively when you are exhausted. Therefore, it is imperative you get rest, even if it is just fifteen or twenty minutes a day.

Many moms tell me (and I've said it before too) they do not have the time to think for themselves. That brings me to my next point. You must make time to think. If you get completely wrapped up in your children and do not take the time to think, the enemy will constantly tease your mind with hopeless, defeating thoughts.

For with God nothing shall be impossible.
Luke 1:37 KJV

Exercise is likewise important. I have not really struggled with long-term weight issues, and I think that may be why I don't take my exercising regime too seriously. But when I view it as serving God and my family better, then I am more inclined to exercise. The benefits of exercise are tremendous, and we can do simple things like an exercise video.

We can be too sacrificial as moms so that we neglect our appearance. I have been guilty of that more than I care to confess. I used to buy floral blouses just because the flowers hid the baby-food stains. Or, as a homeschooling mom, I'd constantly be looking like an Oscar Madison reject because I reasoned we'd be doing some messy science experiment. I've learned that I feel better when I dress better.

Determine what you will do on any given day, and let your outfits reflect that decision. When my children were very little, I used to give myself dress-up days. Even if I was not going anywhere, I would get dressed up that day and not do any heavy cleaning. Those were the days I'd devote myself more to prayer. Since I was dressed fairly nicely, I was not tempted to go mop the entire kitchen floor just because some applesauce fell on it.

Eating right and personal hygiene are also important. It's the little things we do that add up to major things. We should have healthy snacks in the house so we aren't tempted to eat the potato chips.

Taking Care of Your Soul

Our minds also need ministry. I am going to assume no one is watching daytime serials or trashy talk shows.

Schedule reading time. Our family has a quiet time in which we read. I pray and read during my quiet time. Audio books are excellent for busy moms, as are audio magazines. Invest in good parenting books and stay on top of child development so you'll know what to pray for by the stage your child is in. This was easy when my children were preschoolers, but it took a bit more work to find adequate resources for older children.

Get out and do things with like-minded mothers. Pray and talk. If your church or community does not have such a group, consider starting one. You may find ministry in your own need. Journal. Journaling is a great therapeutic exercise, and you may use it to probe your own thoughts, talk to God, or write letters of love and adoration to your children.

Invest in your marriage. Do not get so obsessed about serving your kids that you neglect your husband. Many times women look to have their needs met by their husbands but do not stretch to understand the men in their lives. I always tell moms who come up to me to complain about their husbands, "You cannot pray for someone whom you are judging." Ask God to cleanse your heart so you can sincerely pray for your husband to be blessed because you want the best for him, not because you want the residual blessings. Attend marriage meetings, and regularly get together with other couples who also value their marriages. Stay away from those who do not value their marriages or families, as it will begin to affect you. Do not assume you are strong.

Taking Care of Your Spirit

Reading the Bible is essential to spiritual growth and understanding the character of God. You may get the

I have overcome the world.
John 16:33

Bible on cassette and listen in your car, while you're cooking or playing with the kids, or almost anywhere. Get an easy translation. I like *The Daily Bible* (NIV), which has the Bible reading separated into bite-size chunks so it's easy for me to read. Derek reads *The Once a Year Bible* to the kids and accomplishes his reading goals and spends time with the kids at the same time. I have enjoyed reading Bible storybooks to my children because they are so simple. This usually spurs me on to go read my Bible for myself.

Meditating on Scripture is essential. We meditate on Scripture when we mull over it until it changes us. We reflect on it, memorize it, and search for ways to apply it to our lives. As moms, it's imperative that as we do make time to sit down to read the Bible, we meditate, because that brings the greatest benefit.

Quiet yourself when you first rise before you even get dressed for the day. Learn to be quiet. Practice silencing your distracting thoughts by exercising concentration. Refuse to think on distracting thoughts. If the thoughts persist, give them over to God. Set a goal to be quiet for a brief time.

Read the Scripture slowly, asking yourself and God questions. Memorize Scripture. Slowly repeat it to yourself. Ask the Lord how you may apply the Scripture to your life. Pray the Scriptures back to God. Biblical meditation—taking the Word of God into us—displaces the sin in us. As we walk in the Spirit, we do not fulfill the lusts of the flesh. Our spiritual self-image is important. We must know God is well pleased with us.

Growing in the Love of God

I feel most unqualified to write this portion, as I know I still struggle with the love of God. I know that he is real and that his love is not some kooky kind of feeling, but resting in his love sometimes seems difficult. I think it's because I'm so performance oriented and receive praise and recognition even from myself when I am doing something.

I read a book that asked, "What do you think God would say of you if he was talking to the angel Gabriel?" At that moment I didn't think God was pleased with me. I had been slack in my quiet time and short with my children and husband. I felt bad, and the more I thought about it, the worse I felt. Then God spoke to my heart and said, "Cheryl, you never asked me what I thought about you." The truth was, I was afraid to ask him; but in fact, he wasn't angry with me. He loved me.

Our relationship with God is not based on assumptions. His love is steadfast. God does not just love. He is love. This is a hard concept to fathom. The essence of his being defines who he is. I have heard sermons about growing in the love of God, and I think I finally understand it. I can only love my neighbor in the love of God to the degree that I am free of myself.

As we die to ourselves, we grow more in the love of God because we become more like God. Therefore, as moms, our spiritual growth is essential to our children's well-being. As much as we love them, it is with a selfish love. This is not condemning, as God has placed a love in us for our children; but that love can never be compared to the love of God.

The love of God for a long time was such an abstract term to me. In many ways it still is. But every day I am growing to understand that God loves through me even before I lay myself on the altar and let him remove wrong attitudes,

213

How to Take Care of Your Spirit

- Have quiet time.
- Journal frequently.
- Meditate on Scripture.
- Pray always.
- Seek God daily.

viewpoints, and activities from my life. I joy in this process, because as I press in to know him better, I am becoming more like him—for we become whom we behold. The only way to grow in the love of God is to submit ourselves to getting to know him better every day.

Develop a Passion for Prayer

There are many books on prayer, and this book has been conspicuously void of any direct teaching on prayer. This was not an accident. There are so many good books that address the different kinds of prayer—petition, supplication, praise, thanksgiving, the pattern of the Lord's—that I would be remiss to think I could duplicate the prayer anointing of those who have pressed into the prayer process.

Prayer is a personal conversation between you and God, and we have to be careful not to methodize such sacred conversations and thereby lose the vitality and life of the relationship. We should get information on prayer, but we should not regiment our praying. Our own ongoing conversation with God and our desire to know him should guide all our prayer efforts. Try different things. I have found it beneficial at times to write out my prayers to God and his responses.

God's response to us is always favorable. He is on our side. Sometimes guilt and shame keep us from coming

How to Take Care of Your Body

- Exercise.
- Prayer walk.
- Play a sport.
- Take vitamins and/or supplements.
- Get rest daily.
- Get a full night of sleep.

to God, but he wants us just the way we are. The secret to developing a relationship with God is to come to him with reckless abandon as we hunger for his righteousness. When we try to get worthy to come to him, we begin to lean on our worthiness. Be real with God. Talk to him about everything and anything. There is no such thing as being too trivial with the Lord.

Trust God, and in the familiarity, do not lose sight of the fact that he alone is the Creator of the universe. Take him seriously. Document your prayers and the answers. This will encourage you, especially as you review answered prayer. Ask questions—the right questions, ones that reveal how committed you are to God's plan for your life. Do not ask, "Why did this terrible thing happen to me?" Rather, ask, "What can I do since this terrible thing has happened to me?" Do you see the difference? One blames God and fosters inactivity; the other invites God in and demonstrates trust and reliance on the Lord. Trusting God with your life means putting confidence in his ability to be God in your life, even when you don't understand everything that is happening to you at the moment.

All circumstances are subject to prayer. Prayer is proactive. Stand against the victim mentality that says you cannot do anything about what happens to you. You can do something! Prayer changes things. Prayer changes you. Choose an attitude of joy. Mothers can become very overwhelmed by caregiving, and it becomes easy to acquiesce to feelings of inferiority. Do not allow it. First John 4:4 declares that we who belong to God are overcomers, because "greater is he that is in you, than he that is in the world." We must have an attitude, a tenacity, to press in and receive all God has for us.

Our attitude or perceptions determine how we pray. We tend to pray confidently and expectantly when we have an overcomer's attitude. Practice daily confessing the Word of God over yourself and your family. You can do this by posting a daily affirmation, much like you would for your children, as discussed in chapter 9. Luke 18:1 states that men (or women) are always to pray and not faint or give up. We have to persevere in prayer.

Pray for your family. Pray with your family. Never pray at them. Amos 3:3 states, "Can two walk together, unless they are agreed?" (NKJV). The most powerful place of agreement is our agreement with God. When we pray for our families, we can decree God's blessings over them and ask for his intervention. When we pray with them collectively, we come together to take our concerns to the throne. We pray at them when we rehearse their negative points to God and tell how displeased we are with them. Prayers to change others, particularly those close to us, can often be selfish prayers. Even a wife has to pray for a husband to change to the degree that the requested change will yield fruit in his life.

Ask God to cleanse your heart before you pray for your family. Ask him to circumcise your heart as you discipline yourself to daily pray for your family. It takes discernment to move from praying the good to praying the best. It might be good for your son to use his gifts to become a pastor. It might be best for your son to be a missionary to Liberia. It might be good for your daughter to marry and have children. It might be best for your daughter to be God's ambassador to the world.

Develop a Love for Reading the Bible

Reading the Bible is a necessity for a Christian. When our children are young, we have to be creative when it comes to finding time to read the Bible, but this discipline should not be neglected. Dottie Schmitt, popular women's speaker of Immanuel Church in Silver Spring, Maryland, often says, "When we do not have an appetite for the Word, we must ask ourselves what we are snacking on." Moms, sometimes we snack on books, television, friends, self-pity, preoccupation with housework, and so on. Snacks divert our attention from what will really satisfy our hunger.

We simply must cry out to the Lord to help us love reading the Word. Jesus will open up our understanding, for we must have the understanding of the Word and the empowerment of the Spirit (Luke 24:45, 49). It is a good discipline to read the Bible through yearly. The Bible on cassette can prime your Bible reading time, but do get involved in reading the book for yourself. Children will be motivated to read and grow as they see you becoming spiritually mature. Stay with the Word: it will grow you up.

The Bible is our mirror. Once we look into it, we will have to adjust our lives. Bible reading is not a stagnant church tradition; it is a vital, life-giving practice. Our understanding of the Scriptures gets better if we stay in them and by faith believe that God will speak to us through them. As Christians, each time we read the Bible, we are changed; indeed, we repent. Repentance is a lifestyle as we daily agree with God. We cannot sincerely read the Word and continue in our self-centered ways. We must trust God to do

How to Take Care of Your Soul

- Talk to other adults daily.
- Engage in discussions.
- Read stimulating books.
- Memorize Scripture.

the work, and that's why reading the Bible is so important. It has the ability to transform us.

Walking with God

We talk a great deal about God's awesome power and our trust in him. The greater question becomes, can God trust us? Can he trust us to have a good attitude no matter how dark things become? Can he trust us to keep our eyes on him and to walk on water to the other side despite what everyone in the boat is saying? I hope that he can trust me. I want to be a friend of God. I have wanted this for such a long time, especially when I read about Abraham, and I so admire Enoch.

Enoch walked with God. For years, as a Sunday school student and later a teacher, I learned and taught about Enoch. I was and still am so impressed with his relationship with the Lord. After all, he walked in continual fellowship with the Lord. One day the Lord directed me to read Genesis 5:21–22. It says, "Enoch lived sixty-five years, and begot Methuselah. After he begot Methuselah, Enoch walked with God three hundred years, and had sons and daughters" (NKJV). Did you realize that Enoch was sixty-five years old before he began to consistently walk with the Lord? That gives me so much hope. My walk with the Lord can grow more fervent at any moment. Enoch was sixty-five. I can change today and pursue God passionately.

I can repent and make a decision to walk with the Lord today and never turn back. I can be an Enoch. I can be a friend of God just like Abraham. I am a child of God and can enter his presence. I can sit at Jesus's feet. The zeal of the Lord can consume me, such that daily I walk and talk with God even as I serve my family. My persistent faith and prayer can drive me into the presence of God—and so can yours!

There are only two things that will last forever: the Word of God and our relationships.

We can walk in agreement with God. How can two walk together unless they agree? Our hearts must agree with God. Agreement occurs in relationship. We have to spend time with God and hear his heartbeat.

Like the Recabites, we must pass this legacy to our children, for God is a generational God. Relationships will last into eternity, but we must nurture them here on earth. There are only two things that will last forever: the Word of God and our relationships. Our relationships will last into eternity, although they might not have the same human conventions attached. For instance, in heaven there will be no more marriage per se, but Derek and I will still be good friends in heaven. This reality is almost too simple to appreciate fully. One day those of us who love the Lord will not only be like Jesus, but we will be with Jesus.

While we are here on earth, daily, as we behold Jesus and are transformed into his likeness, we must keep eternity in sight. For as we keep our eyes fastened on him, we will walk on water. Yes, moms, we can do the impossible as we pursue God relentlessly, because he is pursuing us! His arm is outstretched to us. He bids us to take that first step. As we draw near to him, he draws near to us. Moms, as we chase after God, we may indeed be delighted to find out he is really not running away from us.

219

Chasing God is obviously a misnomer, because God never runs away from us. He is in hot pursuit of us.

Chasing God is obviously a misnomer, because God never runs away from us. He is running in our direction. In fact, he is in hot pursuit of us. And as we meet one another, we embrace. Receive his embrace now. Feel his full, warm arms comforting you, enveloping you, and removing the pain, the agony, the emptiness of being without him. Talk to him. He is listening to you. He understands. Enjoy him. He likes being with you. Love him. He loves you!

Listen, he is speaking to you. Hear what he is saying. "I love you. Come closer. Come sit with me. I will tell you wondrous things. I will share my secrets. I will renew your spirit. I will give you rest. Come to me. I am here. I love you. Let me love you."

Notice, he smiles as he reaches out and grabs you, and grins—"I caught you!"

Prayer

Lord, renew and refresh me in your presence. I need you, Lord! I want you. Capture me with your love.

12

I Really Want to Know!

Questions We All Ask

Even after reading this book, perhaps you still have questions. Most of us do. These are the kinds of questions we would not necessarily ask in a crowd or where others might hear us. But I think you'll find this chapter one of the most helpful because these questions were compiled from questions moms have asked me over and over. I don't confess to know all the answers, but I will share my heart as God has shown me how to chase him and the kids too.

How can I be a good mom?
You cannot. All our righteousness is as filthy rags. Even what seem like our noblest thoughts may be rooted in pride, bitterness, and so on. We all struggle with pettiness, selfishness, and our own sin nature. Even the things we seem to do right have impure motives. The only hope for our children is to have a mother who is constantly in communion

221

with God. Our children do not need a good mother. They need a godly mother. Submit your life to God and let him so inhabit you that your children see God in you.

Sometimes I don't feel like I love my children or my husband, especially when I have to constantly pick up after them. I feel bad, but I am angry with them all the time. What should I do?

You resent your family. I too used to battle with feeling slavishly used by my family. I would branch out into the "no one appreciates me" lecture when I would pick up dirty towels off the floor or put away toys. I subtly resented my family. Why couldn't they just keep the house clean once I cleaned it? Surely it was a conspiracy to drive me insane. Each time I was confronted with picking up after someone, I would go ballistic inside.

The Lord began to deal with my attitude and showed me I had to be filled up with him and give out love and acceptance even when I was annoyed. The real problem was that I saw my family hindering me instead of seeing myself as a servant for them and, at the same time, a leader. I learned to go to the Lord and have him give me strategies for helping my attitude and keeping the house clean.

I know I should press in to know God, but I feel so overwhelmed all the time. What do I do?

When moms become overwhelmed, the first thing to go is their quiet time or their time alone with the Lord. This is the enemy's strategy. We need to press into God more when we are stressed. Meditate on posted Scripture. Pray right when you are feeling overwhelmed, and expect God to answer you. Be sensitive to his Spirit. He may tell you to lower your cleanliness standards or give up a Bible study—something radical to get you some time to yourself.

My kids are so disobedient. It irritates me. I get so angry even when I have quiet time.

As moms, it is our responsibility to move our children to a place of obedience and self-control, but we must, as the Scripture says, possess "a readiness to revenge all disobedience, when [our] obedience is fulfilled" (2 Cor. 10:6 KJV). In other words, I have to do the right thing before I require it from my kids. Every stimulus offers us the opportunity to respond. It is our job to respond correctly, not in anger or exasperation, if we are to teach our children. The key is accepting the fact that you can't control your children's behavior. You can control your reaction to the behavior, and a well-thought-out response is always more effective than rampant anger.

My children do the most unexpected things. It frustrates me. What should I do?

With children, you should expect things to happen that will put a monkey wrench in your carefully devised plans. I remember that no matter how many times I changed diapers before we left for church, inevitably I had to change a diaper again—just when I was ready to walk out the door. If I accept diaper changing and serving my children as a sacrament to God, I am less frustrated. If I am constantly angry at them because I can't do what I want to do or they don't adhere to my plans, then I communicate conditional love and resentment.

I have to give the service of my family over to the Lord. This is so elementary it almost sounds silly, but stay with me. Jesus places a high value on children. He sees us. Mothering is a great place for Christian service because there is so much you do in private. Often it is those things we do that are just between us and God that make all the difference. Perhaps even in reading this book you might discover just a minor shift in your attitude toward serving your family that can help draw you closer to God.

How can I manage my time?

Time management for moms is really self-management. For mothers, it's keeping on top of things so we can respond to the unpredictable—which will surely come in our day—from a point of reason, rest, and prayer. We cannot calculate when we will have to change the next diaper or deal with the next bout of the stomach flu.

There are a few practical things we can do. Make a schedule. Of course, it will be an ideal schedule, but it will help you to identify the holes in your schedule. Most likely it's the holes in your schedule that are taking up your day. Moms with young children should keep a running list of things they would do if their child took an unexpected nap—and I suspect spending time with the Lord would be on top of the list. I have found scheduling and spending time with the Lord gets easier as your children get older. Toddlers and infants tire you out more quickly than school-aged children, although I'm sure if I caught you on a bad day with your active teens, you might not agree with me. I exerted more physical energy when my children were infants and toddlers, and I exert more emotional energy now that they are older.

"Every crisis is an opportunity for you to learn how to be a better mother." I often parrot these words to myself when I am in the midst of a crisis. I ask, what can I learn from this experience? Next, I ask, how might I avoid this happening in the future?

These two questions are crucial, because motherhood is full of the unpredictable. We can embrace these trying moments as learning experiences or scorn them. Either way, we will have them. It all has to do with our attitude;

and remember, our dominant attitude sets the atmosphere of the home.

Every crisis is to grow us as moms or as Christians. For instance, if your children are constantly spilling their milk at the breakfast table, spoiling their church clothes, and thereby hindering your schedule, then it may be time for you to invest in spill-proof cups.

After you have written your schedule (writing always brings clarity to the process), remember this: be prepared for anything, because anything can happen! I think most of us frustrate ourselves because we do not realize motherhood is not regimented. Tending to another's interpersonal, hygienic, and emotional needs is messy and unpredictable. It requires a lot from us. We must constantly be full of the Lord to give out.

What's the one thing I can do to grow spiritually?

The secret to spiritual growth is following God daily. The truth is that if we follow God daily, we are less likely to make glaring mistakes, because they can be easily corrected. Errors increase over the span of time. When we get off the right path, God has given us time to get a fresh start each day.

Since God wants us to spend all our time with him, all of our time belongs to God. If we miss out on getting in God's presence and getting filled, we are likely to do it all in our own strength. Our strength, even at its best, is weak. Most mothers know this to be true, but few have accepted this fact and sought ways to get filled daily. He is with us always, even until the end of time. We need to acknowledge his presence so we can fully appreciate the blessings of his presence.

What is quality time?

Give your family lots of quantity time, and in the process you will discover quality time. Jesus spent quality time with his disciples. They ate with him; they walked with him. They watched what he did and said. They watched him teach the multitudes, yet they also watched him lift a small child and compare entering the kingdom of God to becoming like him. Jesus is our model for leading our children. Make a commitment to spend quantity time with the Lord and your children.

All time belongs to God. All twenty-four hours of our day belong to God, not just the time we go to church or stop to pray. If we could fully grasp this truth, it would change the way we schedule our day. Too often we schedule God out of our daily plans. We go to work, or wash the dishes, or talk on the telephone as if God were not with us. He is involved in everything.

What's one key to productivity?

We are much more productive after quiet time because it provides us peace. Peace is the prerequisite for productivity. Relaxation is really the key to getting more done. Learn to relax and be at peace first with God, then with yourself. Did you know that when you are upset with yourself, you reflect that onto your children? Be careful about the things you say to your children. You have to be emotionally whole. Ask God to show you the emotional holes in your life. Ask God to heal them.

How can I have quiet time with three preschoolers?

Let's face it, as a busy mom, you probably cringed when you came to the chapter on quiet time, especially if your children have special needs, they were birthed in quick succession, or you're blessed with a busy-beaver child who can defy any child-safety latch. Or maybe your entire Christian walk you've wrestled with devotional consistency. Whatever the reason, you've come to regard quiet time as a chore. I know what you mean, but you have to make it a priority, even if you spend just ten minutes in the morning or during naptime or pop in a video and take time for yourself. Trade time with another mom and pray. Proclaim a quiet time in your house. Little ones can read books, color, or play quietly. Do not accept that you can't have quiet time. It's a matter of your attitude. Do not get perfectionist and think you need to spend long hours in quiet time. A consistent ten minutes is better than no time at all.

What's the difference between Bible reading and meditation?

Bible reading is reading or studying. Biblical meditation is slow, contemplative, and quiet meditation, mulling it over and over in our mouths and minds. We truly have to take the Word of God and keep saying it, singing it, and praying it until we believe it for ourselves.

Getting ready for church is hard for me. What can I do?

A lot of planning. Sunday morning is pivotal for Christians, yet often Sunday morning for the Christian mom is greeted with aggravation and agitation as she argues with children to move faster. Then there are the disagreements over acceptable clothes and a host of other things that cause us to arrive at church exasperated with a praise-the-Lord, phony smile on our face.

We need to arrive at church peaceful and prepared to participate in the praise and worship of our Lord. It doesn't happen if we're fussing with the kids and yelling at everyone and giving them that "holy mom" guilt trip—you know, the lecture we give when we want our cherubs to be motivated by our motherly guilt. Frankly, it doesn't work in my house, and it probably doesn't in yours either. If it did, we wouldn't be delivering it every Sunday morning.

I guess some moms are waiting for me to say that dad should help. He should, but since I'm not speaking to him right now, you can tell him Cheryl said he should help you. Of course, if he hasn't listened to you all these years, what makes you think he'll heed my words?

I greatly appreciate Derek's help with the children, but even his help must begin before Sunday morning. Prepare for church as soon as possible. A week in advance is best. I used to take out my girls' dresses, press them, and choose coordinating tights or socks along with their barrettes. I always tried to keep their church shoes away from them. Likewise, I would press my son's suit and choose a necktie, socks, and shoes. I then hung the freshly pressed clothes back in the closet. Over the years we have made going to church more casual, but I still insist on no holey jeans, faded blouses, or multicolored outfits. Of course, all of these are the fashion trend now, and I laugh at my restrictions but still enforce them. Derek and I believe in keeping a standard, even though church is very casual.

Since I am not totally responsible for my children's clothing, I allow them to get their clothing out Saturday night for our approval. I encourage them to gather all accessories, including hair bows for my girls. Preparing the evening before eliminates the drama in the morning when we disagree on what a child should wear. By the way, ladies, be sure to check with dads. Derek had to point out to me the correct length of a shirt sleeve in relation to a suit jacket as well as the proper knot for a necktie.

Every mom has already discovered that getting dressed first, before everyone else, is the way to go. You still need to coax children to move along, no matter how old they get. Now that my children are all elementary-school age, it has gotten tremendously easier. I have been told that moms of teenagers need to constantly remind them to move along and deal with grumpy attitudes.

Nursing moms and those with infants and toddlers may opt to put on panty hose and undergarments and slip into a dress right before they leave the house. I have also gotten completely dressed and worn my robe over my church clothes. I move faster in slippers. A few times I was almost out the door before I realized I still had my slippers on. And one time I wore two different shoes to church, one blue and the other black.

We have to slow down, not just so we can have matching shoes, but for the sake of our children's spiritual development. If Sunday mornings are rushed and we are ill-tempered, what kind of message are we communicating to our children? Children remember things emotionally. If we want them to serve God and to know he is a loving God, we should do our best to provide a peaceful atmosphere on Sunday mornings. We can do this by being thoroughly prepared.

Everything should be prepared ahead if possible, even breakfast, unless your church service is midafternoon. Set the breakfast table on Saturday night. Also have your children put their church bags by the door. (Our children always have church bags with things to keep them occupied in church or if mom and dad have to attend a meeting.)

How can I balance my church service and parenting?

When our children were young, both Derek and I were in ministries that took a lot of time and commitment. We were part of a fast-growing church and, as a result, spent a lot of time in church. We would sometimes leave the house Sunday morning at six o'clock. During the fall, it was still dark. We didn't return home sometimes until after six in the evening. We were on a tight family budget, and I would have to make breakfast, lunch, and snacks for the kids to have while we were at church. We would eat an unhealthy quick dinner when we got home.

229

Regrettably, this was not God's best for our family and presented in us an inability to see our home and family as our first ministry. We were stressed then, although neither of us fully understood just why. Now that we have understanding, we encourage young families to carefully seek the will of God, especially if both Mom and Dad feel called to the ministry. Whenever you give time to something, you have to take time from someplace else. We all know that, but we sometimes think it doesn't include religious or church service. Involve your whole family in any plan you make for ministry. Also remember that your toddler may not understand the ramifications of a choice you make to serve a ministry. Ask God for wisdom, and be prepared if he says, "No, not now."

What does God require of us as parents?

Jesus always honored parents. When he healed Jairus's daughter, he put everybody out of the room but her parents. In John 4:49–50, Jesus gave the word to a heartbroken father that his son would indeed live. In Mark 9:14–27, Jesus healed a man's son even though the dad confessed he needed help in believing. Yet Jesus strengthened the man by taking a strong grip on this man's hand. Jesus encouraged this man's faith. We have seen how Hannah's prayers brought forth Samuel's conception, and she later prayed for his dedication to the Lord after he was born (1 Sam. 1:27–28). Jesus does not require spiritual perfection, just a yielding to him. He wants us to come to him, because children are a gift from the Lord.

I once heard someone say, "The most hidden command in the Bible is that we should tell our children, the next generation, of the miracle-working, sign-giving, faithful, powerful God we are called to serve." Children need to be told things over and over. Repetition not only makes for obedience; but when we hear something often enough, we start to believe it.

Our children learn best in the context of our lifestyle. My husband and I tremble and pray that what we say when we speak in public is the same thing we say in private to our children. Jesus's disciples were able to believe because what he said and did in public were the same things he said and did in private. We want the same for our children. Once again, it takes sacrifice. It takes dying to one's self so that Christ may live in us. It takes giving our weakness to the Lord so he can make us strong.

Does being a godly mother mean I'll never have time to myself?

Sacrifice and motherhood almost seem synonymous. I think that's true to a large degree, but I love being called Mommy. It's the only title I am truly proud of. You should be too. Does that mean that because you're a mom you are doomed to a life of giving to others? Of course not. "An empty vessel has nothing to pour" is an adage I often use in my time-management workshops to get moms to realize they have to freely receive before they can give. It is imperative that we are nurtured so that we can be nurturing.

How can I take care of my physical needs when the spiritual needs seem so pressing?

Be creative. Attempt to pair the two activities. For instance, if you can't get to the gym, or if you're like me and just don't like going to the gym, then you can get videos. I enjoy Leslie Sansone walking videos. They are perfect for busy moms, especially since they're fifteen- to twenty-minute videos. My kids love Tae Bo, but it's a bit rigorous for me. You may also exercise by walking more. Walk to the library or the bank. You can also pray as you walk. Prayer walking is a concept that's catching on. Once you start exercising, you will feel better. Exercising increases blood flow and helps you think more clearly. Actually, a bit of exercise before prayer will help you to concentrate more. You just have to keep working at it. Pairing spiritual activities with natural ones is fun and creative. For example, pray for the family and different nations when you're cooking.

What is the first time-management technique you recommend?

Make goals and be strong in the decision process. Moms often don't make goals for themselves. They make them for their children and assist their husbands, but they overlook themselves. Get a notebook and ask yourself what you want to do in five, ten, and fifteen years. What things do you enjoy? Start small. What are your hobbies? I know a Christian mom who knits blankets because she enjoys the relaxing rhythm of the knitting; then she gives them away to infants in a neonatal ward at her local hospital.

Being with the kids all the time makes it hard for me to find time with my husband. Any ideas?

My husband and I have an "internal date night" when we can't find a sitter. The kids have to go to their room and may stay up as long as they do not disturb us. We usually talk or share our favorite food (that we don't necessarily want to share with the kids). Moms, you can take that same concept and give yourself time to read, do a craft, or participate in an activity, if you and hubby alternate nights out. Pray and ask God for creative ways to spend time with your husband.

How can I sensitize myself to the Spirit of God in the midst of my busy day?

Pray and ask God to show you creative ways to find time to do the things you love to do. Allow him the gift of companionship, with him to envelop you. Invite God into the time you listen to music. Talk to him about the things you're sewing. I like to discuss with the Lord what I am going to write, and I often feel his anointing.

What's one mistake moms make?

The real reason we do not take time for ourselves is because we don't feel we are worth it. We are worth it.

How can churches help mothers?

Mothering mentors are needed in the church: moms who raised children, who have tenacity for the Lord, and who passed that passion on to their children. Such mentors are truly needed. In fact, while I rejoice at the revival of the men's movement in the church, I am saddened to see so many mothers lacking basic nurturing skills. We erroneously think the nature of a woman makes her a good mother. This is not always the case, especially in a culture that is antithetical to motherhood.

How can we really connect with our heavenly Father?

Consecrate all your time to the Lord. He takes joy in you enjoying yourself, just as we as moms like to see our children have a good time. Jesus was not serious all the time. How do you think he knew the songs children in the marketplace sang? Because he played with them. As we are free to connect with the things that bring us joy and refreshment, we are better equipped to be more responsive to our children and our husbands. When our schedule is too full, we do not even give space for God to get into our day. Our relationship with God is based on the time we spend with him and how we respond to his prompting.

Is it truly necessary to be quiet?

Quiet time is really an inward discipline where we silence our thoughts, desires, and flesh to hear God. In truth, anytime we hear God, we have engaged in our quiet time. The goal of quiet time is meeting with God to be transformed, and anytime this has occurred, it is in essence quiet time—even as you meditate on Scripture that you post on your wall and experience the peace and presence of God. Our goal should be to know God.

How can I have quiet time during the day?

Establish a general family quiet time. Even infants will eventually respond to an environment that is quiet all around them. When you first begin, some of these infants and toddlers may not cooperate; but as you continue to press in to teach your children the discipline of quiet, you will find it's worthwhile. Make goals for your quiet time—not mechanical, lifeless goals like, "I will read the Bible through," but goals focusing on *why* you will read the Bible through. While it's a good habit to regularly read the Bible, add a bit more faith to the process. Ask yourself what you want as a result of reading your Bible through in a year.

Resources

Brother Lawrence, *The Practice of His Presence*. New Kensington, PA: Whitmaker Books, 1982.

Although I still prefer the original form, this updated translation will encourage you to seek God in the ordinary activities of your day.

Carter, Jarrett, Janae, and Jolene. *A Kid's Guide to Organizing*. Long Island, NY: Jehonadah Communications, 2002.

This book, designed for six- to fourteen-year–olds, will help your children to be more organized. It will motivate them to clean their rooms and complete household chores and give advice on living with messy siblings. It is a fun yet practical book.

Available from Foundations for Family Success Ministries, P.O. Box 712, Uniondale, NY 11553, or visit www.momtime .net.

Copeland, Germaine. *Prayers That Avail Much for Mothers*. Tulsa, OK: Harrison House, 2002.

This book is a great guide to jump-start your prayers for your children. I routinely give this book as a gift to new moms. It is very basic, utilizing Scripture to direct our prayers.

Lord, Peter. *Hearing God*. Grand Rapids: Baker, 1988.

This is the best book I've found on hearing God, and it is doctrinally sound. Lord writes in lay terms. Even though I read this book years ago, I still refer back to it often. Lord really takes the mystery out of hearing God's voice. It is so simple yet profound, and you can share certain portions with your children. The illustrations also drive home the points the author makes, thereby making this a good practical read. I learned the concept of FIT from this book: praying frequently, intensely, and over a specified period of time. This book will challenge and change your prayer life. It should be required reading for all.

Mally, Sarah, Stephen, and Grace. *Making Brothers and Sisters Best Friends*. Cedar Rapids, IA: Tomorrow's Forefathers Publishers, 2001.

My kids have read this book many times. Written by three siblings, it is full of practical and godly wisdom concerning family relationships. We cannot recommend this book more highly. Get it for your kids, and read it yourself too.

Sherbony, Steve. *Changing Your Child's Heart*. Wheaton: Tyndale, 1998.

Derek and I read this book a long time ago. It really gets to the center of changing your child's heart and not just dealing with misbehavior. It was a real blessing to us, and we still refer back to it often.

Tozer, Aiden W. *The Pursuit of God*. Camp Hill, PA: Christian Publications, 1982.

I enjoy all of Tozer's writing, but this book in particular challenges my walk with God. He urges the reader to move beyond the superficial into a deeply committed relationship with God. He writes in a way that makes me yearn for a deeper relationship with God. Each chapter, although brief, is full of biblical truth to savor. Tozer remains one of my favorite Christian authors.

Turansky, Scott, and Joann Miller. *Parenting Is Heart Work*. Colorado Springs: Cook Communications, 2005.

Derek and I enjoyed this book because it gets to the heart of parenting issues. It is very practical and easily applicable.

Yates, John and Susan. *Character Matters*. Grand Rapids: Baker, 2002.

This book emphasizes the importance of parents proactively helping their children develop biblical character. It is very practical and an easy read with both a dad's and a mom's perspective.

Recommended Websites

Foundations for Family Success and Organize Your Life!
www.familysuccess.org and www.momtime.net

You will find organizing tips, family advice, and spiritual-growth articles. Visit us and sign up for our monthly e-news-letter. It's full of practical information and spiritual-growth encouragement. See our *Chasing God and the Kids Too* webpage and join our e-discussion list for busy Christian mothers.

Making Brothers and Sisters Best Friends
www.brothersandsisters.net

This website is really great for kids and parents. Their ATTACH program is very practical for even very young children to implement. My kids have applied many of the principles and worked out their own differences so I could have time to pray.

Hearts at Home
www.heartsathome.org

This organization of Christian mothers is working to "professionalize" motherhood. You will find tons of resources.

Mothers of Preschoolers (MOPS)
www.mops.org

This organization addresses the unique needs of mothers with preschoolers.

MemLock Bible Memory System
www.memlock.com

Memlock gives pictorial clues to help memorize particular Scriptures.

Cheryl R. Carter has a passion for God, an excitement for his people, and a joy for the chase. Joining her in the chase are her three school-age children and the only love of her life, her husband, Derek. Cheryl, a homeschooling mom, stirs others in the chase as a freelance parenting writer, inspiring speaker, and leader in the Christian homeschool organization in her home state. She has been doing time-management and organizing seminars just for mothers for over a decade. A self-avowed recovering messie, she likes helping other moms find the freedom of organization so they can better serve their families. Cheryl also assists her husband in Foundations for Family Success, a ministry to today's fast-paced families, where she does preventive counseling, and marriage, parenting, and home education workshops. In her oft-stretched spare time, she relishes spending time with her husband, laughing with her children, and enjoying God in the ordinary. Visit www.momtime.net or www.familysuccess.org for organizing tips and encouragement. Join the *Chasing God and the Kids Too* e-discussion list at www.momtime.net for encouragement, practical tips, and stimulating chat.